Have It Your Way with Feng Shui

As the breeze dances with the wind chimes hanging outside your bedroom window, you smile knowingly … you are in tune with the positive forces of the earth. You are a practitioner of feng shui.

Feng Shui for Beginners presents the ancient art of placement in an easy-to-grasp way so you can put the techniques to use immediately in your home or office. Richard Webster approaches this time-honored tradition in a thoroughly modern and practical way.

Feng Shui for Beginners is the magical place where East meets West. It is your starting point for a healthier, wealthier, and happier life.

You will marvel at how easy it is to rid your home or office of "shars"—straight lines and sharp angles that produce bad luck, misfortunes, even disasters—just by hanging a mirror, moving an end table, or planting a tree.

If abundance is not a part of your life, you owe it to yourself to explore the ancient secrets of feng shui … just follow your heart's desires and the tinkling of the wind chimes.

About the Author

Richard Webster was born in New Zealand in 1946, where he still resides. He travels widely every year, lecturing and conducting workshops on psychic subjects around the world. He has written many books, mainly on psychic subjects, and also writes monthly magazine columns.

Richard is married with three children. His family is very supportive of his occupation, but his oldest son, after watching his father's career, has decided to become an accountant.

To Write to the Author

If you wish to contact the author or would like more information about this book, please write to the author in care of Llewellyn Worldwide, and we will forward your request. Both the author and publisher appreciate hearing from you. Llewellyn Worldwide cannot guarantee that every letter written to the author can be answered, but all will be forwarded. Please write to:

Richard Webster
℅ Llewellyn Worldwide
P.O. Box 64383, Dept. K803-6
St. Paul, MN 55164-0383, U.S.A.

Please enclose a self-addressed, stamped envelope for reply, or $1.00 to cover costs. If outside the U.S.A., enclose international postal reply coupon.

FENG SHUI
for BEGINNERS

Successful Living
by Design

Richard Webster

2000
Llewellyn Publications
St. Paul, Minnesota 55164-0383
U.S.A.

Cover photo: Digital Stock Photography
Cover design: Tom Grewe
Interior illustrations: Carla Shale
Interior photos: Richard Webster
Editing and book design: Amy Rost

First Edition
Sixth printing, 2000

Library of Congress Cataloging-in Publication Data
Webster, Richard, 1946–
  Feng shui for beginners : successful living by design / Richard Webster
  p. cm.
  Includes index.
  ISBN 1-56718-803-6 (pbk.)
  1. Feng-shui. 2. Interior decoration—Miscellanea.   I. Title.
  BF1779.F4W43   1996
  133.3'33—DC20

Llewellyn Publications
A Division of Llewellyn Worldwide, Ltd.
P.O. Box 64383
St. Paul, Minnesota 55164-0383
www.llewellyn.com

Printed in the United States of America

About Llewellyn's Beginners Series

If you're just beginning to explore the many fascinating dimensions of metaphysics, you'll find that the books in Llewellyn's Beginners Series are the clearest and most useful introductory guides around. No prior knowledge of arcane subjects is necessary to understand and apply the techniques in these books. You'll receive a basic overview of the subject and the full range of its uses; practical, step-by-step explanations and instructions for applying your newfound knowledge; and the insider's perspective you need to know in order to grasp the essentials of a given topic—all written for the novice, in plain English.

All of the subjects covered in Llewellyn's Beginners Series are important to gaining a new understanding of our bodies, souls, and vast potential, of nature and our place in the world, and of the immense unexplored regions of microcosm and macrocosm. Whether you use this book as the first step in your quest for personal evolution or whether it's one of many steps in your ongoing journey, you'll find it your best introduction to the boundless possibilities of the metaphysical universe—and of the human spirit.

Other Books by Richard Webster

Palmistry for Beginners

Feng Shui for Success & Happiness

Feng Shui for Love & Romance

Feng Shui in the Garden

Feng Shui for the Workplace

Feng Shui for Apartment Living

101 Feng Shui Tips for the Home

Chinese Numerology

Astral Travel for Beginners

Spirit Guides & Angel Guardians

Aura Reading for Beginners

Seven Secrets to Success

Dowsing for Beginners

Numerology Magic

Omens, Oghams & Oracles

Revealing Hands

Dedication

For two special friends, David and Penny Alexander.

Acknowledgements

Many people have helped me with this book. I would like to especially thank my friend Dr. David Himelrick for sending me valuable information. I would also like to thank T'ai Lau, Charles Hai, Carl Herron, Jon Kealoha, Albino Gola, and Mark Edward for their valuable advice and support.

Contents

List of Illustrations

Introduction

Chapter 1

Chapter 2

Chapter 3

Chapter 4

Chapter 11

Introduction

In 1971 I decided to write a book. It took some three months to write. The first publisher I sent it to accepted it, and the book was duly published. For someone who had always wanted to be a writer, this was a great thrill. I was under way! I had ideas for several other books, but somehow years passed and the books remained as dreams in my head. My second book did not appear for five years. At the time I had every excuse in the world for not writing it. I was busy at work. I had a young family. I had little free time. I didn't realize at the time that feng shui was also involved.

We moved house immediately after I had written my first book, and my desk was placed in an attractive position beside a window overlooking our garden. I would sit at my desk and think about writing, but I never seriously got around to writing anything. Then, in 1977, I changed the layout of my office, and placed my desk against another wall at a ninety-degree angle to where it had been before. I immediately started writing seriously again. At the time I thought it was coincidence, but once I became interested in feng shui and checked the room I discovered that I had unconsciously moved my desk from a negative position to a highly favorable one. This was my first personal experience of feng shui, and it was an accidental one. However, I was already aware of how feng shui had helped friends become happier and more successful.

Several years ago, while enjoying a cup of tea with a friend, I heard a tinkling sound coming from outside her house. I commented on the sound because I knew that she had previously kept her wind chimes in her bedroom.

"I moved them outside last year," she told me. "A Chinese friend told me that it was bad feng shui to have them inside my house."

"The most amazing things have happened to me since I put them outside," she continued. "I was offered a job by someone I met at a party. I accepted the job and on my first day there met the man I am going to marry." She spread her hands in delight. "Everything seems to have improved! I now believe in feng shui!"

My friend's experience is not an uncommon one. As she told me how her life had changed once she improved her feng shui, I recalled a similar experience I had fifteen years earlier with a friend in Singapore. He had been experiencing business problems and consulted a feng shui *xian-sheng* (Mr. Feng Shui) on the advice of a friend. This feng shui expert rearranged his office furniture and suggested that my friend place a yellow ceramic fish on his receptionist's desk. A large mirror was placed in the lobby as well.

My friend rather reluctantly paid the man his fee, thinking that the minor alterations could not possibly do anything for his business, but within a month he was on a sound financial footing again and has gone from strength to strength ever since. Recently, I visited him again. He now has a huge business and owns the office building where he works. Before moving, he consulted the same feng shui expert. This time, he was told to remove the ceramic fish and replace it with a chrysanthemum.

"It might sound crazy," my friend said, "but it works!"

Many people regard feng shui as superstition. For instance, in feng shui, the shape of a hill could indicate a benevolent dragon or a ferocious tiger. An overhanging rock could be a protective tortoise or a bird of prey.

It is believed that any form of earth works can bring bad luck if the underlying dragon is injured. A Victorian traveler, Isabella Bird, reported that coal seams were worked only on a level, as any digging could graze the dragon's back.[1] When the first railway tunnels were being constructed in Hong Kong, Europeans had to be brought in because the Chinese would not risk hurting the dragons and tigers beneath the earth.[2]

Today, all major building projects in Hong Kong still follow the precepts of feng shui. For instance, it is said that one of the five chimneys at the Aberdeen power station was erected purely for feng shui safety, as four is considered an unlucky number.[3]

Many of the hotels in Hong Kong have used feng shui to help achieve success. The Mandarin Hotel in Central has its doors placed at an angle to the street to make it harder for spirits to enter. The Peninsular Hotel, built in 1928 and still one of the most prestigious hotels in Hong Kong, is shaped like a magnet facing the harbour. This enables it to capture positive energy in its outstretched arms.

Hong Kong's Peninsular Hotel is shaped like a magnet to attract positive energy from the harbour it faces.

The nearby Ocean Centre, a large shopping complex, also has a large U-shaped magnet facing the harbour. The building was constructed this way in the belief that it would attract money and good luck to the center. This complex is an extremely busy one. Many hotels in Hong Kong, Taiwan, and Singapore cover any columns in the lobby with mirrors, to avoid any problems caused by sharp edges.

A concern feng shui experts held about the Regent Hotel was handled in an interesting way. There were fears that this large hotel might block views of the harbour from Kowloon. More importantly, there were worries that this new building might prevent the nine dragons from getting to the harbour to bathe (*Kowloon* means "nine dragons").[4] The hotel resolved the problem by building a large glass atrium through which the harbour can still be seen.[5]

There are a number of sites in Hong Kong that feng shui practitioners have always considered to be the best of all. The Hongkong and Shanghai Bank occupies one of these, but all the same, feng shui practitioners were brought in at all stages of its planning and construction to give advice.[5]

Feng shui experts were brought in at all stages of planning for the Hongkong and Shanghai Bank.

Even the positions of the escalators were adjusted slightly to harmonize with the rest of the building. There are many stories relating to the two stone lions, Stephen and Stitt, who rest in front of the building. Feng shui experts were brought in to decide on their correct position.[7] The actual placement had to be done at 4:00 A.M. on a Sunday, and both lions had to be moved simultaneously by two cranes to prevent either animal from becoming jealous. Once in position, the lions were formally welcomed in a ceremony that included having the bank's directors pat the lions.[8]

Feng shui experts determined the best position for Stitt, one of two stone lions outside the Hongkong and Shanghai Bank. Stitt and his counterpart, Stephen, had to be repositioned simultaneously so neither would become jealous.

Some years ago the Hongkong Bank took over the Hang Seng Bank. Believers in feng shui claim that this happened because the entrance of the Hang Seng Bank's head office resembled a huge mouth that was unable to close, letting the money get out. The entrance consists of two large pillars acting as wedges to hold the "mouth" open. The escalators inside the entrance look like teeth, adding to the illusion.[9]

The entrance to the Hang Seng Bank's head office resembles a huge mouth that is unable to close.

Close to the Hongkong Bank is the Bank of China, Hong Kong's tallest building. Interestingly enough, this building was opened on August 8, 1988 (8/8/88). Because the word *eight* means *wealth* in Cantonese, the Communists chose the most propitious day of the century to open their bank. However, some local feng shui experts remain cynical about the bank's long-term success. They say that the shape of the

Some feng shui experts say the shape of the Bank of China is unlucky and its sharp, angled sides create poison arrows of negative energy.

building is unlucky, and the sharp sides create poison arrows of negative energy, some of which seem to be directed inward.[10] The Hong Kong newspapers reported that a willow tree was planted in the grounds of nearby Government House to ward off the negative flow of energy caused by the Bank of China building.[11]

Chinese-born architect Jen Chih-chen, worked for thirty years as an architect in the United States before moving to Taiwan. In an interview,[12] he said that architects in the East need to be very aware of cultural habits, particularly feng shui, to ensure that buildings get oriented the right way, and the rooms are all placed in their correct positions. He considers feng shui requirements to be "very strict." Certainly, many buildings in Taiwan have rounded corners to eliminate any potential lines of negative energy.

Architects around the world are paying more and more attention to feng shui. Even Donald Trump is using the principles of feng shui in his massive Riverside South project in New York City.[13] Not so long ago, this would have been considered eccentric, to say the least. Nowadays, it is accepted as being sound common sense.

Probably the best-known feng shui story in Hong Kong concerns Bruce Lee, the famous kung-fu film star. Once he became famous he bought a villa in Kowloon Tong, a trendy area for the young and successful. However, this area has always been avoided by the older people as it is situated in a valley, and valleys are believed to have bad feng shui. On the advice of a geomancer, Lee had a pa-kua mirror attached to a tree outside his house to improve his feng shui. Unfortunately, this tree was blown down in a typhoon and the mirror was broken. Lee neglected to replace it, making his death at the early age of thirty-two inevitable, according to many feng shui experts. Some people even claimed that the nine dragons of Kowloon were jealous of his success and deliberately killed the "Little Dragon."[14]

A little-known fact about Hong Kong is the existence of "feng shui woods." These are the oldest areas of woodland in Hong Kong and form a barrier to protect many of the villages in the New Territories, the part of Hong Kong that is situated on the mainland. They are usually crescent-shaped and consist largely of native forest trees. They provide, in effect, a large feng shui remedy to hide any lines of negative energy that could affect the villages and their inhabitants. Nowadays, many trees are planted in these woods to benefit the village. For instance, *Aquilaria sinensis* (Joss Stick Tree) is often planted as a raw material in the making of incense. Litchee, Chinese white olive, guava, and bamboo are also frequently planted in these feng shui woods.[15]

The feng shui woods are partly responsible for my interest in feng shui. They are charming, peaceful, restful places that are seldom visited by anyone other than local villagers. I tried to find information on feng shui with little success. The books that were available either approached the subject from a historical point of view or else regarded it as an ancient superstition. None of them offered practical advice that I could use myself.

Fortunately, there are now many books available on the subject, but most of these are either highly technical or concentrate on the history of feng shui.

This book is designed to be as practical as possible. An air of mystery has pervaded the subject and made it incomprehensible to all but the most determined of students. I hope this book will help to change that and make the subject clear and easy to understand. I have studied the subject for many years now and have been able to help many people with it. It is extremely rewarding to see the incredible changes that good feng shui can make in people's lives. I hope this book will help you to improve your life in many different ways, as well. When you live in harmony with the universe, good things flow your way naturally. You will experience happiness, contentment, and abundance. That is what feng shui is all about.

1

What Is Feng Shui?

Feng shui means "wind and water." It basically means living in harmony with the environment. The ancient Chinese believed there was order and balance in the world, and that by following certain actions individuals could attract good fortune to themselves. If we live in harmony with the winds and the waters of the earth, we attract good luck and prosperity. The concept of living in harmony with the environment is a comparatively new idea in the West, but has been practiced in the East for thousands of years.

The origins of feng shui are lost in antiquity, though it is believed to have started some five thousand years ago when Wu of Hsia (2953–2838 B.C.E.) found a tortoise that had a perfect "magic square" in the pattern on the back of its shell. From this chance discovery evolved the I Ching, Chinese astrology, numerology, the Nine Star Ki, and feng shui.[1]

Between 1933 and 1936 Walter Schofield discovered more than one hundred prehistoric sites in Hong Kong. At Tung Wan, on Lantau Island, he found a Stone or Bronze Age burial site where six people were buried with their heads pointing towards the south. As the south has always been considered an auspicious direction in feng shui, this could well be an indication that feng shui was practiced in prehistoric times.[2]

There is evidence to show that at least three thousand years ago government buildings and imperial palaces were built using the principles of feng shui.[3] The city of Canton was established at about this time, using feng shui principles. Today, it is still a beautiful city, lying at the head of the Chu Chiang (Pearl River) Delta, ninety miles from the sea, surrounded by gentle hills.

Beijing has hills in the north to protect it from the cold winds. On clear days it is possible to see the Western Hills from the Forbidden City, the most perfectly created feng shui site of them all. Another precept of feng shui is to have water in front of your home, rather than behind it. The Golden River flowed through the first courtyard in the Forbidden City, following this principle exactly.

Marco Polo recorded that the emperor had constructed a large mound, one hundred paces high and more than a mile in circumference, on the northern side of his palace. This mound served as the Black Tortoise and improved the feng shui of the palace.[4]

The basic principles of feng shui were first written down during the Han dynasty (25 C.E.), though scholars had been theorizing and writing about various aspects of it as early as the Song dynasty (960 B.C.E.).

Over the years small changes were made to the system, but the basic ideas of feng shui have been unchanged since the Tang dynasty when Yang Yun Sang wrote a series of books on feng shui for Emperor Hi Tsang (888 C.E.). Yang Yun Sang wrote extensively about dragons in these works. Even today, dragons are the most revered of all the celestial creatures in China.[5] In feng shui symbolism, green dragons and white tigers lie beneath and form most hills and mountains. The principles of feng shui that Yang Yun Sang wrote about are today known as the **Form School**, one of the major categories of feng shui. The Form School deals largely with the formation and contours of the landscape.

One hundred years later, Wang Chi and other scholars from the Sung dynasty (960–1126 C.E.) researched all of the old classic texts and wrote extensive commentaries on them. Feng shui, as it is known today, is based largely on the research of these Sung dynasty scholars.

Gradually, these scholars began to think that people's individual energy should be harmonized with the celestial energy from the land. Consequently, a second school of feng shui began that used aspects of Chinese astrology, the **pa-kua symbol**, the **Lo Shu magic square**, and the **luo-pan compass** to work out the best locations and directions for individual people. This system became known as the **Compass School**.

Feng shui has always been considered one of the most important areas of life. An ancient Chinese saying lists the five basic principles of successful living: "First comes destiny, and then comes luck. Third comes feng shui, which is followed by philanthropy and education."

Destiny is determined by our horoscope, which outlines our path in life. It reveals our strengths and weaknesses. We should capitalize on our strengths, of course, and work on improving areas of weakness.

Luck is a difficult word to define. The Chinese believe that we can improve our luck by working on the other four principles. Luck is largely a state of mind. If we look to the future with anticipation, rather than fear, and expect good things to happen to us, events will usually happen the way we want.

The third principle is feng shui. Using this we can live in harmony with the world and everyone in it. Living this way will improve every aspect of our lives, including luck.

The fourth principle is philanthropy. The ancient Chinese philosophical and religious texts say that we should give with no thought of any reward. Selfless giving in this way provides its own special satisfaction, and is guaranteed to improve the quality of our lives.

Finally, there is education. We should all try to improve ourselves as much as we can. Education should be a lifelong exercise, and we should try to keep as up to date as possible with what is going on in our world.

Some versions of the saying list effort rather than education as the fifth principle. Naturally, we need to expend effort for anything to happen. Hard work is essential for any degree of success in life.

Ch'i

The ancient scholars believed that in the universe there was originally just one abstract energy known as **ch'i** (the breath of nature). This is often referred to as the dragon's celestial breath. Ch'i is an invisible energy that circulates everywhere, but gathers in certain places, which are said to be good in feng shui. Because ch'i brings happiness, prosperity, and longevity, it is avidly sought after. The Chinese believe that ch'i enters new life at the moment of conception. Ch'i is the life force inside all living things, and can be found in its perfection whenever something is done perfectly. For instance, an artist creating a magnificent portrait, or a boxer hitting a perfect punch, are both creating ch'i.

Conversely, when someone is feeling ill or lethargic they are said to be lacking in ch'i energy. We need beneficial ch'i to be active and healthy. Someone who is always enthusiastic and ready to tackle new projects is full of ch'i. In this instance, ch'i would flow upwards through the body creating an aura effect around the top of the head. This aura can grow and diminish, depending on the vitality and health of the person. Ch'i can be increased by meditation, good relationships with others, a healthy lifestyle, and good feng shui.

In feng shui we are looking for places where ch'i accumulates or forms as this is the perfect place to live happy, prosperous, successful lives. Ch'i is easily scattered by strong winds. Consequently, windy sites are not good from a feng shui point of view. However, when ch'i is bounded by water, beneficial ch'i usually accumulates. This is why the people of Hong Kong regard their harbour as the source of their wealth. The exits from the harbour are also small, allowing the wealth to be held inside. (Many people are concerned that the massive reclamations that are taking place in Hong Kong harbour today will adversely affect the levels of ch'i and take away or reduce the colony's wealth.)[6]

However, not all water is beneficial. If it flows too fast it will take the wealth away. If it flows in a straight line it will also carry away the ch'i energy. The water ideally needs to be slow-moving and meandering.

It is important to choose a site where ch'i energy can build up and accumulate, or alternatively, where new ch'i is constantly created. These places will always be beneficial. A site surrounded by slow-moving water and rolling hills to dissipate the winds is ideal.

In feng shui mythology, the first time ch'i moved it created **yang** (the male principle). When it rested, **yin** (the female principle) was created. After creating male and female, ch'i went on to create the entire universe. The theories of yin and yang are vitally important in feng shui.

The other important elements in feng shui are the **eight trigrams** that were found on the back of the tortoise shell, and the **five elements** of fire, earth, wood, water, and metal.

Yin-Yang

Yin and yang are regarded by the Chinese as being the balancing, harmonizing factors of the universe. They are opposite energies and neither could live without the other. In fact, yin energy can always be found inside yang, and vice versa as the white spot (yang) inside the yin and the black spot (yin) inside the yang of the popular yin-yang symbol testify. Lao Tzu said, "A single Yin cannot be born, and a single Yang cannot be grown."

Yin and yang are normally pictured inside a circle creating the Taichi symbol of completeness. The yin, the yang, and the circle are the three elements of the symbol that become one. *Taichi* means the "supreme, the ultimate" and derives from the two words *tai* and *chi*. *Tai* means the greatest, and *chi* means the utmost.

The etymology of the words *yin* and *yang* is interesting. Yin signifies the shady, northern side of a hill, while yang signifies the sunny, southern side.

Yin and yang together make up *Tao*, the way. Everything in the universe is made up of yin and yang energies. They constantly interact with each other.

Yang is active, masculine, dominating, and positive. It is full of power and energy. Yin is receptive, feminine, yielding, and negative. It supports, nurtures, and sustains. Yang is day, and yin is night. There are many other examples to represent yin and yang, such as heaven and earth, night and day, black and white, female and male. One cannot exist without the other. For instance, without night there is no day, and without death there is no life. The Chinese delight in collecting opposites to represent yin and yang energies.[7] Although the Chinese enjoy doing this, they are also aware that it can be overdone. "Yin yi tou, Yang yo tou" ("one face in yin and one face in yang," which means to hide one's real intention) and "Yin yang guai qi" ("strange yin-yang airs," which means to act strangely) are also popular Chinese sayings.[8]

The ancient sages never tried to fully explain the concept of yin and yang, preferring to allude to it in poetic words. After all, ch'i energy is the life force and it created the duality of yin and yang. It simply is. Neither yin nor yang can be evil or good. They just are.

In feng shui, hills, mountains, and other raised areas represent yang energy. Valleys, rivers, and streams represent yin. Earth that is completely flat is said to contain too much yin. An extremely hilly landscape with no water or plants would be described as being too yang. Gently rolling countryside represents a good balance of yin and yang.

We can achieve balance of yin and yang using feng shui. For instance, we could introduce plants, rocks, and buildings to a flat landscape. We would need to be careful doing this as small trees grow into bigger trees, and this can ultimately affect the feng shui of the immediate area.

The concept of yin and yang applies even in death. A yin house is for the dead while a yang house is for the living. Because ancestor worship is an important part of Chinese life, it is not surprising that feng shui is involved even after someone has died. It is believed that the correct placement of the grave has an important influence on the success of the descendants.

For instance, the Chinese believe that the astonishing success of Sun Yat-Sen at the turn of the century was caused by the perfect feng shui placement of his mother's grave.[9] Chiang Kai-shek's success was also attributed to the placement of his mother's grave. His downfall began when the communists dug up the grave.[10]

As a result, there is a whole branch of feng shui related to determining not only the best burial place, but also the most propitious day in which to conduct the funeral. Ideally, a burial ground should be undulating, as this relates to the body of a dragon. The dragon symbolizes the Superior Being. Flat ground symbolizes a "false dragon," while undulating ground represents a "real dragon."

If possible, the burial ground should face south. The Chinese believe that the dead need air to breathe, and south-facing ground provides the "breath of cosmic life," which is very favorable. The Chinese believe that a lack of this cosmic breath would adversely affect the fortune of the person's descendants, making selection of a suitable grave site exceptionally important.

Finally, the tomb has to be oriented in the right direction. This is determined from the birth date of the person being buried. By consulting a luo-pan, or geomantic compass (which will be discussed in Chapter 5), the correct direction is determined.

The graves must be well looked after to ensure that good fortune remains with the descendants. On All Saints Day the descendants visit the graves of their ancestors and clean them thoroughly. It is a bad sign if the grave changes color. A blackening of the grave is a portent of disaster, and white indicates a time of mourning for the family. Usually, a red powder is placed on the grave stones to try to avoid the possibility of whitening or blackening.[11]

We will be dealing almost entirely with yang houses (houses for the living) in the rest of this book.

The Taoist symbol of the universe is the yin-yang surrounded by the eight trigrams (Figure 1A, next page). This symbol, known as the **pa-kua**, is extremely popular in the Far East, and can be found in temples, palaces, shops, and houses.[12]

Figure 1A: The pa-kua.

The Eight Trigrams

The Chinese people believe that the eight trigrams of the I Ching represent the secret of life. The eight trigrams were devised by Wu of Hsia, and come from the four symbols known as Ssu Hsiang that represent all the possible combinations of yin and yang (Figure 1B). The lower row of these figures determines whether the symbol is yin or yang. These four symbols were doubled by adding an extra line to them, creating the eight trigrams (Figure 1C, page 12). These trigrams are doubled up to create the sixty-four hexagrams used in the I Ching. However, in feng shui we use only the sixteen trigrams, and do not need the hexagrams.

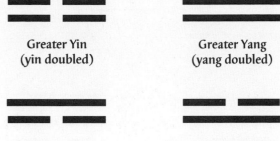

Greater Yin
(yin doubled)

Greater Yang
(yang doubled)

Lesser Yin
(yin changing to yang)

Lesser Yang
(yang changing to yin)

Figure 1B: The Ssu Hsiang.

The I Ching, or Book of Changes, is the oldest book of China, and quite possibly the oldest book in the world. It is by far the most important of the Wu Jing, the five ancient Chinese classics. Its effect on Chinese thought, philosophy, and culture is incalculable. It was written to help people understand and handle change, and to lead successful, fulfilling lives. It described the universe as an entity, with everything inside it moving and changing. It helped people become attuned to the endless cycles and rhythms of nature.

The entire universe is moving and changing all the time. Life is a progression of change, from birth to death. The I Ching can provide valuable advice and help for people at every stage of life. Both Taoism and Confucianism derive their philosophies and beginnings from the I Ching. Fortunately, the I Ching survived Emperor Chin Shih-Huang's Great Burning of Books in 215 B.C.E., the only Confucian text to survive.[13]

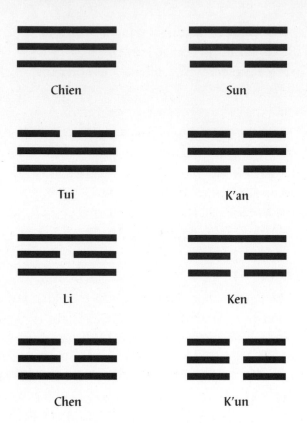

Chien   Sun

Tui   K'an

Li   Ken

Chen   K'un

Figure 1C: The eight trigrams of the pa-kua.

The Pa-Kua

The pa-kua (pronounced par-kwar) is an octagonal symbol that depicts the eight points of the compass. South is always at the top, following the Chinese compass. Consequently, north is at the bottom, east to the left, and west to the right. The eight trigrams of the I Ching are placed in position at each of the eight directions. It is believed that the trigrams give the pa-kua its power and energy.

There are two different combinations of the trigrams, the Former Heaven Sequence and the Latter Heaven Sequence. The Former Heaven Sequence (often known as the Hsien Tien) was devised by Wu of Hsia and depicts an idealistic, perfect picture of the universe. The Latter Heaven Sequence (often known as the Hu Tien) was devised by the Duke of Wen, founder of the Chou Dynasty in about 1143 B.C.E., and depicts a more practical arrangement of the trigrams. Consequently, the Latter Heaven Sequence is the more useful arrangement for feng shui, allowing its energies to influence the earth's ch'i.

The Latter Heaven Sequence is derived from the Lo Shu diagram, which was originally discovered by Wu of Hsia on the shell of a tortoise. It depicts a perfect three by three magic square, the numbers of which total fifteen in every direction, vertically, horizontally, and diagonally. The yin, odd-numbered trigrams take the cardinal positions with number five in the middle. The yang, even-numbered trigrams take the sub-cardinal positions.

In feng shui, the Lo Shu magic square using the Latter Heaven Sequence is placed over a person's home and indicates the best locations for each member of the family. It also shows the best locations for each room to enable the occupants to live in peace and harmony. This system of feng shui is part of the Compass School and is known as the Flying Star.

The Five Elements

Everything in the world, according to the Chinese, belongs to one of the five elements of fire, earth, wood, water, or metal. These elements are believed to affect everything we do. There are five different ways in which ch'i energy can be manifested.

In our horoscopes we have most or all of the five elements. The quantity of each element determines our personalities and degree of success in life. It takes a highly skilled astrologer to successfully balance and interpret the effects of these five elements in our horoscopes.

Wood

Wood is creative and innovative. If we have a large amount of this element in our charts, we will express ourselves creatively in some way. Wood can be pliant and bending (willow) or strong and unyielding (oak). Wood is sociable and community minded. Wood also represents the color green, the season spring, and the direction east. Wood also represents birth and early childhood. In the eastern part of the Forbidden City in Beijing the buildings were covered with green tiles, because they housed the young princes.

Fire

Fire gives energy and enthusiasm, but can also be a sign of danger. When too much fire is present, it can be destructive. Fire warms and cheers, but it can also burn and destroy. Fire is the element of the natural leader. Fire represents red, summer, and south. Fire represents the growing years before puberty.

Earth

Earth gives stability and also relates to real estate and legacies. Earth is patient, just, honest, and methodical. However, it can also be smothering and demanding. Earth represents the color yellow, the center, and the teenage years.

Metal

Metal (also frequently referred to as "gold") indicates harvest, business, and success. This is usually financial success. On the negative side, metal can also indicate a sword or a knife and be destructive and violent. The color is usually white, but can also be gold. It symbolizes autumn and west. Metal represents the adult years. In the palace at Beijing, the empress had her quarters in the western wing and the walls were painted white.

Water

Water indicates travel, communication, and learning. It also relates to literature, the arts, and the media. Water can be both gentle (soft rainfall) and violent (a hurricane). Water nourishes all living things, but can also gradually wear away the hardest rock. It represents the color black, winter, and north. Water represents the final years, old age.

Cycles of the Elements

There are three cyclical relationships between each of the five elements. The first of these is known as the **cycle of production** or the cycle of birth (Figure 1D, page 16).[14] If we start at the top and go around clockwise, we can see that fire produces earth (ash). Earth is strengthened as fire is weakened. Earth, in turn, creates metal (minerals), strengthening

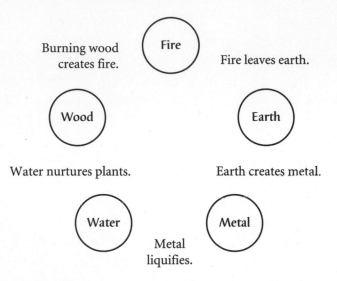

Figure 1D: The cycle of production for the five elements (also known as the cycle of birth).

metal and weakening earth. Metal then evolves naturally into water. Consequently, water is strengthened by metal at the same time as the metal is weakened. In the same way, water leads on to wood (trees and plants). Here the wood is strengthened and the water weakened. Finally, we can burn wood to create fire, weakening wood and strengthening fire. This is also known as the Early Heaven or Fu Hsi (or sometimes Wu of Hsia) arrangement.

There is also a cycle of destruction (Figure 1E) that shows which elements overpower others. For instance, fire dominates metal, because the heat of the fire can melt it. This is a negative situation that creates an imbalance. The metal

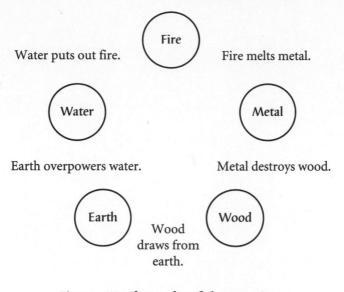

Figure 1E: The cycle of destruction
for the five elements.

destroys wood. The wood destroys earth and the earth over-powers water. Finally, water quenches fire. This is also known as the Latter Heaven or King Wen arrangement.[15]

Finally, there is also a cycle of reduction (Figure 1F, page 18). This cycle is used to correct any imbalances caused by the destruction cycle. We know from the cycle of destruction that metal overpowers or destroys wood. In the cycle of reduction water is placed between metal and wood and serves to neutralize the potentially destructive effects. Like-wise, fire overpowers metal in the cycle of destruction. In the reducing cycle, earth is placed between them as earth puts out fire and reduces the overpowering effects.

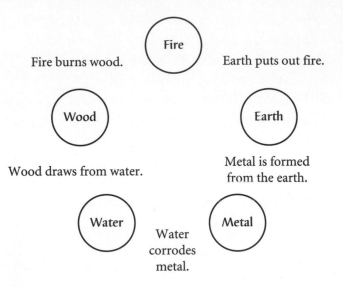

Figure 1F: The cycle of reduction for the five elements.

Following the cycle of birth allows difficulties to be resolved peacefully. The cycle of destruction does the opposite and always creates problems. The reducing cycle neutralizes the effects of the cycle of destruction.

Your personal element is determined from your year of birth. The next most important element comes from your time of birth. You can determine these using the tables "Elements and Signs for the Years 1900 to 2000" and "Element at Time of Birth," located in the Appendix (pages 161–164). Once you know these two elements you can see if they harmonize together, are neutral, or try to destroy each other. For instance, I was born at 4:50 P.M. Consequently, the element for my hour of birth is water. I was born in 1946, a fire year. Fire and water are destructive, as water quenches fire. I can counteract this destructive effect by using wood (as wood is between fire and water in the reduction cycle).

Problems can sometimes arise when someone has the same element for the year and the hour. This creates an overabundance of the energy that can work against the person's best interests. In practice, when this happens a much deeper investigation is made to determine the person's elements for the birth month and day.[16]

Many Asians deliberately choose their children's names using the five elements feeling that this will give them an added edge in life. For instance, if someone is born in a fire year, the parents will choose a name that incorporates wood, as wood creates fire.

In feng shui we want the interior of your home to be as beneficial to you as possible, so we try and harmonize your personal element into your surroundings. For instance, I was born in a fire year, so I would benefit from having plenty of wooden or green objects, such as plants, around me. This is because wood creates fire. By the same token, I should avoid black objects and too much water, as in the destruction cycle, water destroys fire.

All of this gets complicated when more than one person lives in the same house. In this case, the elements of the head of the house should be used in all of the main rooms, while the bedrooms and other individual rooms should reflect the element of their occupants.

Finally, to achieve peace, wealth, happiness, and contentment with feng shui, we need to find a place containing abundant ch'i, a good balance of yin and yang, and a harmonious balance with our personal element.

2

The Form School

Much of feng shui has to do with common sense and observation. The ancient Chinese noticed that life was easier living on the sunny, southern slopes, surrounded by rolling hills to dissipate the harsh winds. They noticed that the hills and rocks looked like strange animals, and they saw that some of these seemed protective while others looked threatening. It must have been very comforting, for instance, to know that your home was protected by a green dragon. A triangular shape is less comforting. Pyramid Hill, overlooking the settlement of Ichang in China, exactly replicates the size and dimensions of the Great Pyramid in Egypt. The local geomancers believed that it adversely affected the feng shui of the area, so a monastery was built on the opposite side of the river, where priests prayed to try and ward off the harmful influences of the hill.[1]

The Form School is a branch of feng shui that analyzes the shape and contours of the landscape. Dragons are very much a symbol of China. In the Form School of feng shui, dragons are raised land forms, but they are not easy to find.

A dragon is not beneath every hill. Feng shui experts carefully analyze the countryside, observing the contours, the foliage, and even the color of the earth. Where a dragon is found, there will also be a white tiger.[2] The dragon and the tiger usually create a horse-shoe shape, with the dragon lying on the east side and the tiger on the west. The hills of the dragon are slightly higher than those of the tiger.

Particularly fortunate sites would also have black tortoise hills to the north and red phoenix hills to the south, creating animal symbolism in all four directions (Figure 2A).[3] A gently flowing, meandering river is also required.

This position is an extremely favorable one. There will be gentle breezes, lush vegetation, and an abundance of ch'i energy. Some feng shui masters say they know as soon as they are in the presence of ch'i because the air smells fresh and clean.

The greatest amount of ch'i energy is found where the loins of the dragon and tiger are joined together in intercourse. The dragon is male, providing yang energy, and the tiger is female, providing the necessary yin energy.

A house built on this site would provide wealth, health, happiness, and abundance for everyone who lived there. Obviously, only one house can be built in this position, but there are many more places where abundant ch'i can be found. The areas around the dragon's heart and stomach are particularly good.

An example of an ideal feng shui site is the Ming Tombs, sometimes known as the Shi-san Ling (Thirteen Tombs), which house the graves of Emperor Yung Lo and his descendants. The emperor's tomb sits in the center of a semicircle

Figure 2A: Fortunate feng shui sites have animal symbolism in all four directions.

of hills, while his descendants rest in graves in auspicious sites in the hills. The hills to the east are known as the Azure Dragon Hills, and the White Dragon Hills are on the west. It is a perfect feng shui site.

Conversely, the dragon's tail and head are bad sites. It would be potentially dangerous every time the dragon moved its tail, and the head is also risky as you might site yourself too close to the dragon's mouth and be eaten.

The perfect site we have just described is known as "The dragon protecting pearl" in the ancient texts. In this site ch'i is able to gather and grow. An area with strong winds could never be a good feng shui site as the ch'i would quickly dissipate, carrying away all the good luck and wealth with it.

The dragon's lair is never found in a windy position, or where there are straight hills or rivers. Fast-flowing rivers and streams carry away good fortune. The rivers need to be slow-moving and meandering to allow the ch'i to build up. Ch'i accumulates near slow-moving water. Fast-moving waters and strong winds carry it away. Remember, feng shui means "wind and water." The right amount of water is always necessary to create a good feng shui site.

Of course, the water needs to be good water. Polluted or stagnant water creates poisonous ch'i that needs to be avoided. Sometimes this poisonous ch'i can be eliminated by cleaning blocked drains or getting rid of accumulated refuse. However, if the water cannot be kept clean, it is better to move house.

Homes built close to meandering streams, rivers, and other water courses will always be happy and prosperous. This was the theme of the Water Dragon Classic, a famous feng shui text that was written about 600 C.E. This text contains many illustrations showing where houses should and should not be built. The water dragon is pictured in the shape of the river and its tributaries, and the best spot to build is in the area of the dragon's stomach. It is often better to build alongside a tributary or inlet because the main river often travels too quickly, carrying away the beneficial ch'i (Figure 2B). Another good position is where two streams or rivers meet. However, they must meet gently, rather than violently, so that the ch'i can gather.

Figure 2B: River inlets or tributaries bring beneficial ch'i to a home.

It is believed that the water dragon can fly up into the air and become a sky dragon (a cloud). The clouds eventually turn to rain and the water returns to the earth again, ready to start another cycle.

Naturally, a house perched on top of a hill is not likely to be a fortunate one from a feng shui point of view. It would be exposed to all the winds and any water would flow away. Both of these factors dissipate valuable ch'i.

Of course, there are many things we can do to our environment to improve our feng shui. This needs to be done with a great deal of thought to avoid angering the dragons, and adversely affecting the flow of beneficial ch'i. Even temporary changes can have an effect. Many new subdivisions start by removing all the vegetation, leaving ugly scars. However, once the houses have been erected, and new trees and shrubs planted, the ill effects disappear. The ch'i may actually increase if the work has been done wisely.

There are many things we can do to enhance our surroundings to either hide negative aspects or increase the effect of good ch'i. We can plant a row of trees to act as a wind break or to avoid the negative effects of a straight river. A wall can serve the same purpose. We can install a pond or fountain to give us beneficial water. Hong Kong contains countless fountains. It seems that every small park has one. This provides beneficial water to create ch'i.

Water also represents prosperity and money. Chater Park in central Hong Kong has a fountain and pond with many tortoises in it. Tortoises are a symbol of longevity, so this peaceful spot in the middle of a bustling city provides for its citizens not only a place to regain ch'i energy, but also a wish for prosperity and a long life.

Water is the dragon's favorite element, creating good ch'i, as well as status and wealth.

Shan

Shan is the term used to describe the different shapes of hills and mountains. Elevated land is desirable because it is the home of the celestial dragons. However, one hill or mountain can be very different than another, and it is important to know which types are compatible for you.

There are five main types of mountains: conical, square, round, oblong, and ridged.

The conical mountain contains a peak that rises up to a sharp point. This is normally a source of bad ch'i, particularly if your home is facing it. It relates to the element fire and the planet Mars. Consequently, people born under metal should not live on this type of mountain. However, people born in an earth year would prosper in this location.

The square mountain contains a large, flat summit. It represents the element earth and the planet Saturn. People born under the element water should avoid living here, but it would prove advantageous for people born in metal years.

Round mountains are narrow and steep, but round off at the summit. They relate to the element wood and the planet Jupiter. It is a beneficial location for people born in fire years, but should be avoided by people born under the element earth.

Oblong mountains are gently rounded. They have a wide, broad base and gentle slopes. They relate to Venus and the element metal. They provide excellent locations for people born in water years, but should be avoided by people born under the element wood.

Ridged mountains appear to have a number of summits like sharp teeth. Rather than a single mountain, they often appear to be a series of mountains. Ridged mountains relate to Mercury and the element water. They are beneficial for people born under the wood element, but negative for people born in a fire year.

Shars

Shars are often known as "poison arrows." There are many potential shars, or negative influences. Shars are created by straight lines and sharp angles that produce poisonous ch'i. Shars produce bad luck, misfortunes, and other disasters. This is because spirits are believed to travel in straight lines and consequently make use of shars. Power lines, railway tracks, walls, rivers, and roads can all be poison arrows when they travel in straight lines. The road that leads to the famous Ming tombs near Beijing curves to the east so that poison arrows will not hit the tombs.[4]

Obviously, it is better to avoid these shars in the first place when moving house, rather than try to correct them later. Fortunately, there are things that can be done if you are faced with a shar, but it is better to spend a little bit more time and find the most suitable house you can, rather than accepting one with damaging shars.

One of the most common shars is to have a corner of a neighbouring building pointing at your house like an arrow head (Figure 2C). A similar shar is traffic traveling on a road aimed directly towards your house (Figure 2D). The intensity of the shar is increased if this road runs downhill

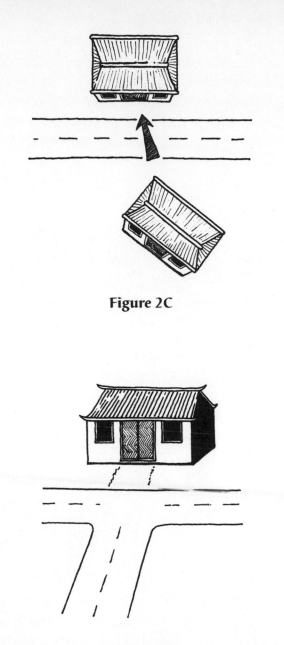

Figure 2C

Figure 2D

towards you. Both of these are made worse if the shar is pointing directly at your front door.

Houses built at the intersection of two streets are considered bad, especially if one of the roads runs in a north-south or an east-west direction (Figure 2E). Even houses built on the curve of a road are believed to attract negative energy (Figure 2F).

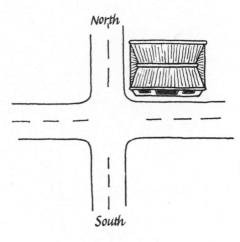

Figure 2E

Figure 2F

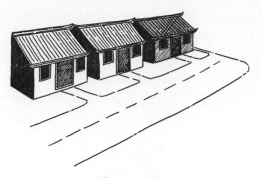

Figure 2G

Figure 2H

The last house in a dead-end road is unfavorable from a feng shui point of view. This is because it is considered that most of the beneficial ch'i will have been used up by the houses at the beginning of the road, leaving very little for the end house (Figure 2G).

A row of trees blocking the entrance to the house is considered a shar. This is because the trees symbolize joss sticks lined up on an altar, making the house and the occupants sacrificial lambs (Figure 2H).

A house facing a factory with tall chimneys has the same shar, as the smokestacks also symbolize joss sticks. A large hill or mound in front of the house is a shar that creates significant financial obstacles for the occupants (Figure 21).

Figure 21

Shars can come in other forms as well. If a building across the road reminds you of a fierce animal, for instance, it is regarded as a shar. A range of hills can be a shar if it is pointing directly at you.

A car park in front of a residential house is considered bad, as any ch'i present becomes stagnant. A car park in front of a store or other type of business is considered good, though, as it allows customers free access to the premises.

Other bad locations include those facing a cemetery, prison, hospital, casino, or police station. These are all places where negative energies gather, and their bad vibrations adversely affect any houses facing them.

Even the fence around your property can be a shar if it consists of many large square holes, like a fishing net. This symbolizes entrapment, and makes forward progress very difficult. Other fences that should be avoided are ones with triangular tops to the pickets. This triangle is considered to be a fire shape, and can lead to quarrels and disagreements amongst family members. Fences that look like a series of tombstones should also be avoided, as they are inclined to attract spirits, who create negative ch'i. Many Spanish-style homes have fences of this sort.

Do not place your clothesline in front of the main entrance. It slowly "strangles" the occupants, impeding progress in every area.

Even a child's slide or swing can be a shar if it is facing the front door. Billboards or extremely large buildings on the other side of the road are also indicative of bad luck. Even worse are two large buildings side by side with a narrow space between them (Figure 2J). If this space forms an arrow

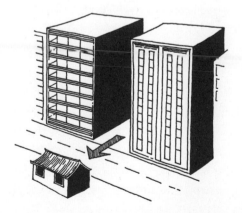

Figure 2J

pointing at your house, it is extremely bad feng shui. In fact, this occurrence is known as "thunder striking from the heavens" as it is believed that bad energies from the sky will flow through the gap and attack the house across the street.[5]

These are all known as physical shars. Remember, they do not necessarily mean that anything bad will happen to people who live in these locations, but the potential is always there. Feng shui energy changes over time. These positions are biding their time until the wrong feng shui placement occurs, then disaster will happen. Rather than be there when this happens, it is better to find a more suitable location in the first place.

Fortunately, there are different ways to dissipate most shars. You can hide a road pointing at you by planting trees or bushes. However, do not plant a tree directly facing your front door, as this is also considered to be a shar.

Some shars cannot be eliminated and the only remedy is to move house. A home sited near an airport that is directly in the flight path of many planes will contain much negative ch'i that will ultimately affect the health of the inhabitants. It is particularly bad for people who are not mentally or physically strong.

A home sited near railway lines is another example. Every time a train goes by, the foundations of the house are shaken, causing instability in the areas of health, wealth, and love. High tension wires create strong energies that affect many people, sometimes causing life-threatening diseases, such as cancer.[6] Rather than wait and see if these negative energies will affect you or your family's health, it is better to move as quickly as possible.

Choosing Land

Many factors come into play when choosing the right location in which to live. Obviously, we need to find a site that has an abundance of ch'i, and fits in well with our particular element. The yin and yang aspects have to be well balanced. Finally, we need to look for any potential shars. These can be natural as well as man-made.

Today, most people live in cities, rather than in the countryside. If you are searching for a home in a suburban area, become familiar with the shapes of the hills around you, and look for potential dragons and other shapes. While you are doing this, also look at any streams, rivers, harbours, or other waterways. Make sure that they are gently moving and are not stagnant.

Check the vegetation in the area. If it looks lush and healthy it means there is good drainage and sufficient water and sunlight. This is a sign of good ch'i.

Ensure that your property gets sufficient sunlight. In China people like to have their houses facing south to allow as much sun as possible to warm the house.

Look also at the roads. Are they straight or gently curving? Avoid locations where the roads create shars. Also avoid situations that are windswept as strong winds carry away beneficial ch'i.

If your piece of land slopes, the back of your house should be higher than the front. This allows the ch'i to flow gently down towards the front of the house. Naturally, if the slope is too steep, the ch'i will disappear down the hill.

Avoid hilltops, unless a nearby higher range of hills provides shelter and protection. If this is the case, ensure that your front door does not face the larger hills. In fact, if possible, have your front door on the opposite side of the house, as it is always better to have the higher hills behind you.

The shape of your plot of land is also extremely important. The ideal site from a feng shui point of view is either square or rectangular. Triangular and L-shaped sites are much more difficult to deal with, but feng shui remedies are available.

The house should be sited on the property so that the front and back yards are similar in size. This creates balance and harmony, essential requirements for good ch'i. Bad luck can come if either the back or front garden is extremely large compared to the other.

If you have bought the land and are about to build, you can ensure that all the feng shui aspects are taken care of before you start. This is easy if the section is square or oblong in shape. If the shape is unusual, it can be made to look more regular by the use of outside lights on top of poles. This is a common remedy in Taiwan. Ponds and waterfalls add to the ch'i, as do musical wind chimes. Imaginative use of boulders and rock gardens can simulate dragons, increasing feng shui and making life more pleasant for the occupants. Good landscaping of the gardens can do a great deal to improve the feng shui of a property. This can also hide negative influences, such as power or telephone poles.

The entrance to the house is also important. The driveway should be curved or meandering. A straight driveway heading directly to the front door is very bad as it creates a shar of negative ch'i. Driveways should also not be narrower at the street end as this has the effect of limiting money. If you have a driveway like this, a light on each side of the driveway will eliminate most of the negative effects. Driveways should not be too narrow or wide compared to the house, but should balance and harmonize the home. Driveways should not slope downwards away from the house as money and good luck will flow away. If you have a driveway like this, ensure that your front door faces away from it. This removes the effect of this shar.

Gardens and shrubs planted alongside the driveway are very beneficial and serve to bring ch'i energy into the house.

Walls and fences can do much more than merely delineate the boundaries of a property. They can be used to hide or block shars. If you have a stagnant stream next to your property, a wall will conceal it from your view and eliminate the harmful negative ch'i. Brick walls need plants and shrubs near them to provide the right balance of yin and yang.

Fences should be chosen with care. Wrought iron fences with spikes or arrows should be avoided. If any of these point towards the house they become negative shars, sending daggers towards you. Downward-pointing arrows indicate downward movement, which eliminates forward progress and could lead to disaster.

Choosing a House

For most of us, buying a home is the most expensive purchase we will ever make. It is vitally important that we choose a home that will be well suited for our needs and also contains plenty of beneficial ch'i.

As mentioned earlier, the best-shaped houses from a feng shui point of view are square or rectangular. Other shapes create feng shui problems that have to be corrected.

An L-shaped house, for instance, gives the appearance that something is missing. This creates financial problems for the occupants. This problem can be alleviated by erecting a light on a pole at the position the house would have been in if it had been square or oblong in shape.

A U-shaped house also gives the impression that something is missing. This shape creates marital and relationship problems. To alleviate this, the "missing area" should be fenced in with a wall that has a pa-kua or mirror placed on it. This wall does not need to be high. Its purpose is to symbolically finish off the house (Figure 2K).

The windows of the house should be rectangular and open outward. This allows ch'i to flow in easily, and provides the occupants with good luck. Windows that open inward stifle opportunities, and this can prove damaging to

Figure 2K: A low wall will symbolically finish off a U-shaped house.

careers. There should be a maximum of three windows to every door in the house.

Windows should not look out onto potential shars. Poles, church spires, the roof angles of nearby houses, and a road heading directly toward the window are all instances that should be avoided. If necessary, keep the window closed and place something in front of it to hide the shar.

Inside the House

The rooms should all be in proportion to the rest of the house. It is bad ch'i, for instance, to have a house with an enormous living room and tiny bedrooms. The rooms should be regular in shape and the ceilings need to be of sufficient height. The rooms need to be looked after and appear fresh. This applies even to door handles working properly and windows opening smoothly. If the house is kept in good condition, an abundance of ch'i will be present.

The living rooms should be larger than the bedrooms. The reason for this is that bedrooms contain yin (female) energy and the living rooms yang (male). In feng shui, even in these days of equality, the male should always be the more dominant one.

The living room should not be on a higher level than the dining room or kitchen. This is because it is the room used for entertaining visitors. If the living room is higher, the ch'i from the house will flow to the visitors rather than the people who live in the house. Single-level floors create and contain much more ch'i than split-level floors.

The front door is of extreme importance and the wrong placement can destroy all the other beneficial aspects of the house. The door should be in correct proportion to the rest of the house to create the correct balance of yin and yang. It should not be attacked by shars, such as roof angles from nearby houses or a steep driveway heading directly towards it. Poison arrows such as these can be eliminated by planting shrubs or plants, or erecting a screen to conceal the shar.

The front door should be wide and open into a bright, cheerful-looking room. This can be a separate entrance hall, but it should offer a view of the interior of the house. The entrance should be as open as possible to allow beneficial ch'i to enter easily. Dark or narrow entrances deter ch'i and make the house gloomy and unappealing. This can be averted by installing lights and a large mirror. The front door should not face a window directly, as it is believed that open windows allow the good energies to escape before they have been around the entire house.

The house must contain a back door. It is dangerous to live in a house with just the one entrance and exit. Ch'i tends to stagnate in this situation and stifles wealth, health, and happiness.

The inside doors should all be of a similar size. Three or more doors in a straight line are considered bad as the arrangement allows the ch'i to come in and then go straight out again. This is especially critical if one of these is the front or back door. Ideally, one of these doors should be blocked off. If this is not possible, a screen placed in front of one of the doors will force the ch'i to flow around it. Another remedy is to place mirrors on some of the doors.

The layout of the house should be designed to allow ch'i to flow effortlessly throughout the house. Straight lines promote negative ch'i, so doorways, arches, and other openings should never be placed in a straight line.

The interior of the house should be bright and well lit. Dark rooms allow the ch'i to become stagnant. This is why gloomy-looking houses often have a strange feeling to them. Chandeliers are favored by feng shui masters as they not only provide an abundance of light, but also contain crystal to amplify the light and enervate the ch'i.

Dark-colored ceilings create bad ch'i as they symbolize a dark cloud overhead. This portends bad fortune as it does not allow the ch'i to circulate freely.

Anything made of wood should have the grain in a vertical direction. It is very bad feng shui to have the grain going in another direction as it takes away wealth. Conversely, prosperity is increased when the wood is in the same direction it was when growing as a tree.

Desks and beds need to be placed against a wall. The occupants lose power and authority if their desks and beds are in the center of the room. If they are standing by themselves in the center of the room they are said to be "floating" and in the "coffin position." This tradition goes back to the days when the Chinese placed the coffins of their deceased relatives in the center of the temple yard while waiting for a suitable burial site to be chosen.

I had a striking example of this with the eleven-year-old son of a friend. He had placed his desk in the middle of his bedroom in imitation of his father's desk at work. Ever since doing this his school work had suffered and his parents were concerned. I suggested that they move the desk back to its original position, and immediately the boy's school work improved. Incidentally, the father was so impressed that he changed the position of his own desk at work and within three months received a promotion.

Beams

Exposed beams create negative ch'i. They impede financial progress and create stress and tension. Sleeping under an exposed beam is especially bad and can lead to headaches, dishonesty, and bad luck. For these reasons it is also very bad feng shui to site a desk or chair directly below an exposed beam.

Stairs

Whenever possible, staircases should curve gently and open onto a wide hall. The stairs themselves should be wide and rounded. Spiral staircases are very bad, particularly if sited near the center of the house. It is also bad feng shui to have stairs opening onto and facing the front door. This allows ch'i to escape out the door.

Staircases should be solid. Those made from individual steps allow money to escape. Staircases should always be well lit to allow the ch'i to flow smoothly.

Toilets

The Chinese are naturally modest and prefer their toilets to be concealed. Consequently, toilets must not directly face front doors, dining rooms, living rooms, or offices. A toilet facing a front door is believed to flush away all of the ch'i that enters the home. The same thing occurs even when the toilet is at the end of a long hallway with doors in between. The doors to toilets and bathrooms should be kept closed.

Kitchens

The kitchen should be as close to the dining room as possible. Family problems can arise if these two rooms are far apart. The kitchen should be light and airy. As this is where the food is prepared, ch'i should be allowed to flow in as unimpeded a manner as possible. Windows, fresh air, color, and light all encourage beneficial ch'i.

The position of the stove is extremely important as it is related to the health and prosperity of the occupants. Ideally, it should face towards the center of the house as this will increase the family's prosperity. If it faces towards the front door the family's health and financial well-being will suffer.

Dining Rooms

Dining rooms should be spacious. Round tables are preferable to square or oblong ones. A large mirror that can reflect the food on the table is very beneficial, as in effect, it doubles the amount of food available. This helps create feelings of wealth and abundance. Illustrations of food on the walls also symbolize abundance.

Bedrooms

It is common in many Western homes for the bedrooms to be placed in a line along a passage. This creates negative ch'i for two reasons. The long hallway, being a straight line, creates negative ch'i. Many doors opening onto the passage create antagonism and frustration.

3

The Compass School

The Compass School contains eight houses relating to the eight trigrams surrounding the pa-kua (see Figure 1A, page 46). This is an octagonal symbol that contains the yin-yang in the center. Around the yin-yang are placed the eight trigrams from the I Ching. Each trigram relates to a different compass direction. The Chinese show south at the top of the pa-kua. Consequently, north is at the bottom, east is to the left, and west is to the right.

The trigrams are placed in position in an arrangement known as the Latter Heaven Sequence. As mentioned in Chapter 2, there are two important arrangements of the trigrams. The first, known as the Former Heaven Sequence (also known as the Hsien Tien), was the original sequence devised by China's first emperor, Wu of Hsia (2953–2838 B.C.E.).[1]

About 1143 B.C.E., the Duke of Wen, founder of the Chou Dynasty, created another arrangement known as the Latter Heaven Sequence. (This is often known as the Hu Tien arrangement.)[2] While the original Former Heaven Sequence is a depiction of a perfect universe, the Latter Heaven

45

Sequence depicts a more practical arrangement of the trigrams for the real world in which we live. Consequently, it is the Latter Heaven Sequence that is more usually used in feng shui.

The Latter Heaven Sequence places the trigram Li in the south, K'an in the north, Chen in the east, and Tui in the west. Sun is in the southeast, K'un in the southwest, Chien in the northwest, and Ken in the northeast.

South

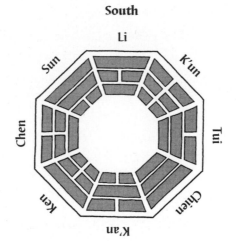

Figure 3A: The Latter Heaven Sequence.

The Latter Heaven Arrangement puts the trigrams into position to provide a cycle of an entire year. We start in the east with Chen (the Arousing), which indicates spring, and everything that promises—new life and great potential. This is followed by Sun (the Gentle) in the southeast; small animals grow during this time. Li (the Clinging) in the south position indicates summer, but shows that the new life is not quite ready to leave the home. K'un (the Receptive) in the southwest indicates the earth and good nourishment. Tui (the Joyful) represents the start of autumn. It is a happy time, but there is a gradual awareness of the approach of winter. Chien (the Creative) in the northwest represents late autumn; it symbolizes the endurance that will be required in the approaching winter. K'an (the Abysmal) represents winter, hard work, and the potential of danger. Finally, Ken (Keeping Still) in the northeast denotes late winter and the end of the cycle.

This cycle could also represent a single day, with Chen indicating daybreak and Ken early the following morning.

The Individual Trigrams

Chien — The Creative

Symbol: Heaven
Keyword: Strength
Element: Sky

Chien consists of three unbroken (yang) lines. It is in the northwest position and relates to the head of the family, usually the father, and to the rooms he would be likely to use, such as the study, den, office, or main bedroom. It represents late fall and early winter. It is strong and indicates energy and perseverance. It also represents heaven. The animal associated with it is the horse, representing power, stamina, and strength.

K'un — The Receptive

Symbol: The Earth

Keyword: Obedience

Element: Earth

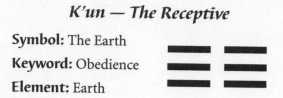

K'un is made of three broken (yin) lines. It is in the south-west position and represents the maternal qualities. Conse-quently, it relates to the mother and to rooms that are traditionally related to the female, such as the kitchen, sewing room, and other places where the mother would be likely to spend her time. It represents summer. It symbolizes the relationship between the husband and wife, but can also be used to represent the relationship between a master and servant, or father and son. It also represents earth (mother earth). The animal associated with it is the cow (usually with a calf), which symbolizes fertility.

Chen — The Arousing

Symbol: Thunder

Keyword: Progress

Element: Wood

Chen is made up of two broken (yin) lines above an unbro-ken (yang) line. It is in the east position and represents the eldest son. Consequently, his bedroom should be in the east side of the house. It represents early spring, and relates to decisiveness and sudden, unexpected happenings. The ani-mal associated with it is the dragon soaring heavenward. This is why Chen is often associated with thunder.

Sun — The Gentle

Symbol: Wind

Keyword: Penetration

Element: Wood

Sun is made up of one broken (yin) line beneath two unbroken (yang) lines. It is in the southeast position and relates to the eldest daughter. Her bedroom should be located in this part of the house. It represents late spring, and relates to wholeness, a good mind, and inner strength. The animal associated with it is the cock, who wakes us in the morning with its shrill "cock-a-doodle-do!"

K'an — The Abysmal

Symbol: Water

Keyword: Entrapment

Element: Water

K'an is made up of one unbroken (yang) line between two broken (yin) lines. It is placed in the north position and relates to the middle son. His bedroom should be in the north side of the house. K'an represents winter, and relates to ambition and drive. Hard work is associated with it, but it can also relate to craftiness and deceit.

Li — The Clinging

Symbol: Fire

Keyword: Magnificence

Element: Fire

Li consists of a broken (yin) line between two unbroken (yang) lines. It is in the south position and relates to the middle daughter. The south is a good position for her bedroom. It relates to early summer, and represents beauty, laughter, warmth, heat, and dryness. It also relates to brilliance and success.

Ken — Keeping Still

Symbol: Mountain

Keyword: Pause

Element: Earth

Ken consists of two broken (yin) lines beneath an unbroken (yang) line. It is in the northeast position and relates to the youngest son. His bedroom should be in this part of the house. Ken relates to late winter, and represents solidity, stability, and consolidation. It can also relate to solitude and instinctive action.

Tui — The Joyful

Symbol: Mouth

Keyword: Joy

Element: Lake

Tui consists of two unbroken (yang) lines beneath a broken (yin) line. It is in the west and relates to the youngest daughter. Her bedroom should be in this position. Tui relates to autumn and represents happiness, joy, pleasure, and satisfaction. Tui also relates to a small lake, which nurtures and refreshes everything around it.

Using the Pa-Kua

It is believed that by orienting your personal ch'i, derived from your year of birth, to the ch'i of the universe you will achieve perfect harmony in your environment, creating an abundance of good fortune.

By using the pa-kua, every house can be related to a trigram. People also relate to the trigrams depending upon the year of their birth. You will be most happy in a house that relates to the same trigram as you. For instance, a Li house favors a Li person, and a Ken house is harmonious for a Ken person.

Your Personal Trigram

You can determine which of the eight trigrams you belong to by looking at the table "Personal Kua for the Year of Birth" in the Appendix (pages 165–166) or using the method outlined in Figure 3B (next page).

Determining Your Personal Pa-Kua Trigram

Here is an easy formula to determine what trigram belongs to any person.

For a man, you subtract the last two digits of his year of birth from 100, and then divide by nine. We ignore the answer, but use the remainder to determine the person's trigram. If there is no remainder the person is always a Li.

For a woman, you subtract four from the last two digits of the year of birth and then divide by nine. Again if there is no remainder, she is a Li person.

- If the remainder is a one, the person is a K'an.
- If the remainder is two, the person is a K'un.
- If the remainder is three, the person is a Chen.
- If the remainder is four, the person is a Sun.
- If the remainder is five, the person will be a K'un if male, and a Ken if female.
- If the remainder is six, the person is a Chien.
- If the remainder is seven, the person is a Tui.
- If the remainder is eight, the person is a Ken.
- If there is no remainder, the person is a Li.

Figure 3B

The Trigram of Your Home

Once you have determined your personal trigram, you can determine the trigram to which your home relates. This depends on which direction the back of your home faces. (In feng shui this is known as the direction in which the back sits.) For example, a Li home faces the north and has its back sitting to the south. A Ken home faces southwest, and its back sits to the northeast. Figure 3C shows the trigram a home would correspond with given its sitting and facing directions.

Symbol	Name	Back sits	Front faces
☲	Li	S	N
☷	K'un	SW	NE
☱	Tui	W	E
☰	Chien	NW	SE
☵	K'an	N	S
☶	Ken	NE	SW
☳	Chen	E	W
☴	Sun	SE	NW

Figure 3C: A home's trigram is determined by its sitting and facing directions.

Now you can compare your personal trigram with that of your home. A Li house would be perfect for a man who was born in 1964 as he is a Li person. The Ken house would suit a woman born in 1957, and a K'an house would suit a man born in 1936.

If the trigram of your home does not match your personal trigram, do not despair. You may still be living in a home that is favorable for you.

The East and West Four Houses

The trigrams can be combined into two groups: the East Four Houses (Li, K'an, Chen, and Sun) and the West Four Houses (Chien, K'un, Ken, and Tui). The trigrams in the East Four Houses group belong to three of the five elements: fire, water, and wood. This is because water gives birth to wood, which then gives birth to fire, making these three elements a highly compatible, harmonious grouping. Likewise, the trigrams of the West Four Houses group belong to the elements earth and metal, which is also harmonious since earth gives birth to metal.

You are most likely to be happy in a home that belongs to the same grouping as you. For instance, if you are a Chien person, you will be happiest living in a Chien home. However, you would also be very happy living in a K'un, Ken, or Tui home as they all belong to the West Four Houses group. You would also be most successful living in a home that had a front door that opened to the west.

Likewise, someone from the East Four Houses group would be happiest in a home with the front door facing towards the east. In fact, it is believed that if you are living in a home that is facing the wrong direction for you, you are risking bad luck, ill health, and financial and marital difficulties. Fortunately, as we will see in Chapter 6, there are wind chimes, plants, fountains, and other remedies you can use to alleviate the negative aspects of living in the wrong home.

Now we come to a difficult question. The average home usually has a number of people living in it. What happens if two of them come from the East Four Houses group and another belongs to the West Four Houses? In practice, the home is assessed by comparing its trigram with that of the major breadwinner. Individual rooms can be arranged according to the primary people using them.

It is considered very fortunate if a husband and wife belong to the same group of houses. This is because the same directions and positions in the home will be perfect for both. (This is just one factor in determining compatibility with Chinese astrology. To determine compatibility properly, complete astrological charts need to be constructed.)

Positive and Negative Directions

Every home can be divided into eight areas determined by the pa-kua directions and the way the home sits. Four of these areas are good locations, while the other four are bad. For instance, in a Tui home, which sits west and faces east, the west, southwest, northeast and northwest are considered positive directions. The east, north, southeast and south directions are considered negative. The positive and negative directions for each type of home are shown in Figure 3D on the next page.

House	Chien	K'un	Ken	Tui	Li	K'an	Chen	Sun
Sitting towards	NW	SW	NE	W	S	N	E	SE
Positive Directions								
1. Prime	NW	SW	NE	W	S	N	E	SE
2. Health	NE	W	NW	SW	SE	E	N	S
3. Longevity	SW	NW	W	NE	N	S	SE	E
4. Prosperity	W	NE	SW	NW	E	SE	S	N
Negative Directions								
5. Death	S	N	SE	E	NW	SW	W	NE
6. Disaster	SE	E	S	N	NE	W	SW	NW
7. Six Shar	N	S	E	SE	SW	NW	NE	W
8. Five Ghosts	E	SE	N	S	W	NE	NW	SW

Figure 3D: Eight areas of a home, as determined by the Latter Heaven Sequence.

1. The **Prime** location is good. The position shown here is always the same as the direction the house sits towards. It is also known as *Fu Wei* (meaning "good life"). This is the area where the back of the home is sited, and it is suitable for beds and doors. It is believed that if your bedroom is situated in this area you will have more male descendants than female ones. (Even today, this is considered beneficial in the East.) Feng shui remedies, such as an aquarium, in this area protect you from bad luck.

2. The **Health** location is good. It is also known as *Tien Yi* (meaning "celestial doctor"). This area brings vitality and good health. It also provides you with good friends. It is a good position for the master bedroom, dining room, and doors. This location should be stimulated to help anyone suffering from a long-lasting illness or poor health.

3. The **Longevity** location is good. It is also known as *Nien Yi* (which means "a long life with many rich descendants"). This area brings peace, harmony, and good health. It is a good location for the bedrooms of elderly people and the dining room. This area of the home should be stimulated when the family is not in accord, as this will help to eliminate disagreements and marital difficulties.

4. The **Prosperity** location is often called *Sheng Chi* (meaning "generating good ch'i"). This is the most auspicious location in the home. It represents progress, promotion, financial success, and vitality. It is a good location for the front door, the kitchen door, the study,

or a desk where accounts and financial matters are taken care of, and anything else related to health and/or prosperity. When this area is stimulated, financial matters will improve. In fact, in feng shui it is believed that if this location is looked after you will ultimately become wealthy.

The direction indicated by your Sheng Chi is your most fortunate direction. If you can orient the most important things of your life in this direction, while at the same time avoiding shars, your success is assured. You can do this by having your bed pointing in this direction, having your front door opening onto it, and traveling to work or business in this direction.

5. The **Death** location has an unfortunate name and is related to accidents, illness, and other misfortunes. It is also known as *Chueh Ming* (which means "total catastrophe"). It is a good place for the toilet. (All of the negative locations are good positions for the toilet as the bad ch'i can be "flushed" away.) This is the worst location in the home, and your front door should never face this direction. It is believed that if your front door does face this direction your family will suffer ill health and you will risk losing all your money and good reputation.

6. The **Disaster** location is related to disputes, arguments, legal problems, and anger. It is frequently known as *Ho Hai* (which means "accidents and danger"). It is suitable as a storeroom, pantry, or toilet. Your bed should not be aligned in this direction as you will constantly suffer small mishaps if it does.

7. The **Six Shar** location relates to procrastination, loss, and scandals. It is also known as *Lui Shar* (meaning "six deaths"). This could lead to legal problems and ill-health. It is a good location for the kitchen or toilet.

8. The **Five Ghosts** location relates to fire, theft, and financial difficulties. It is also known as *Wu Kuei* (meaning "five ghosts"). Like the Disaster location it is suitable for use as a storeroom or toilet. If your front door faces in this direction you could suffer from fire and theft.[3]

Remember to sit facing one of your four favorable directions when doing anything important, such as signing papers, making decisions, studying, or negotiating. The Chinese are famous for their interest in gambling, and many of them make sure that they sit in the Prosperity direction when placing bets. Fortunately, there is an easy way of determining good locations. If your home belongs to the East Four Houses group all four of the east directions would be good locations for you. Likewise, if your home belongs to the West Four Houses group all of the west four directions would be beneficial for you.

For instance, if you live in a Li home, which is one that faces north, and has the back towards the south (referred to as "sitting south"), the directions and locations that are positive for you are south, north, east, and southeast. (These are the directions to which the backs of all four members of the East Four Houses group sit.) Likewise, if you live in a West Four House, the positive locations and directions are northwest, southwest, northeast, and west.

Let's look at another example in detail. Say you have a Tui home, the plan for which is shown in Figure 3E. A Tui home faces east and sits west. With a pa-kua placed over the home we can see the meanings of the positive directions. In a Tui home, the west, southwest, northeast and northwest are the positive directions (Figure 3F). The master bedroom is situated in both the southwest and west directions. These directions cover Health and the Prime locations. This is the perfect location for the master bedroom, unless, perhaps the inhabitants were wanting a daughter. (This is because the Prime location is believed to produce more male babies than female ones.)

In the northeast direction we have the dining room, which in this home is in the Longevity location. This is the perfect position for the dining room, providing a harmonious, happy family life.

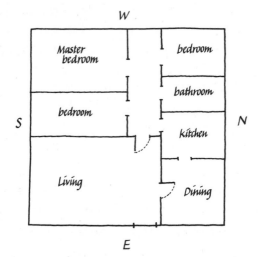

Figure 3E: A Tui home.

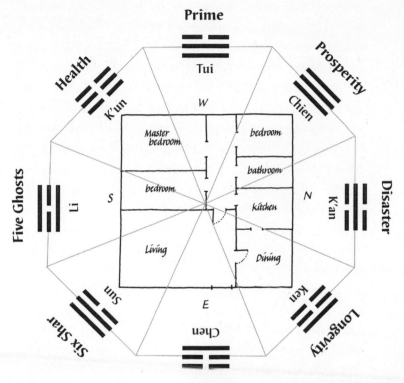

Prime

Tui

Prosperity

Health

K'un

Chien

W

bedroom

Master
bedroom

bathroom

Five Ghosts

Li

S

N

K'an

Disaster

bedroom

kitchen

Living

Dining

Ken

Six Shar

Sun

E

Chen

Longevity

Death

**Figure 3F: Positive and negative directions can also be
determined by laying the pa-kua (Latter Heaven
Sequence) over the floor plan.**

In the northwest we have the Prosperity location. Unfortunately, in this home we have a bedroom in this position, which means that much of the potential of this fortunate direction is wasted. It would be easy to rectify this, though, by placing a desk in this room and using it when paying accounts or undertaking financial transactions. An even better solution would be to turn this room into a study, if possible. That way, the inhabitants would be able to make the most of the Prosperity location in their home. Even worse than this is the fact that part of this location is in the bathroom. This effectively means that a large part of the occupants' wealth will be going down the toilet. A feng shui remedy will be needed here to avoid this.

As already noted, the west direction is the Prime location. At first glance, it would appear that this area is wasted as most of it is taken up with a hallway. However, this area is good for bedrooms and doors. The hallway of this home contains six doors, and the Prime location, itself, covers a small part of three bedrooms.

So far we have covered the positive directions. There are also four negative directions. In this home the south direction is the Five Ghosts location, which covers one bedroom and a small part of the living room. The Five Ghosts location relates to theft and fire. The inhabitants will need to ensure that the windows in these rooms are kept securely locked when the home is empty. They should also avoid using candles or open flames in these areas.

The southeast direction contains the Six Shar location. The living room is sited here. The Six Shar location relates to procrastination and potential loss. Any financial planning should be done in the bedroom in the Prosperity location, rather than in the living room. In this home, the living room would be a place of idle chatter and gossip. The inhabitants would be inclined to make great plans in this room, but never quite get around to carrying them out.

The east direction in this home is also in the living room. This is the Death location. This is the worst position in the home to place the front door, and in this home, that is exactly where it is situated. This puts the inhabitants at risk of losing wealth, prestige, and health. The inhabitants will need to use feng shui remedies to avoid the negative influences. It would be even better if the front door could be shifted into the Prosperity location, which looks to be an unlikely possibility in this home.

Finally, we have the north direction, which in this home is the Disaster location. The kitchen is sited here and the inhabitants would continually argue and squabble in this room. People doing the food preparation in this home would also need to take more than usual care to avoid accidents.

This home is a typical example. It is rare to find an existing home where every room is sited in the most positive location. Fortunately, feng shui remedies can go a long way to eliminate any potential difficulties.

The pa-kua will need to be "stretched" if the home is not square shaped. This means that the pa-kua will become oblong in shape to accommodate the shape of the home. It is believed that square and rectangular homes have the best feng shui, because when the pa-kua is placed over a plan of the home, each trigram section is of similar size. Consequently, a long, thin, rectangular home does not naturally have the same good feng shui as a square home (Figure 3G, next page).

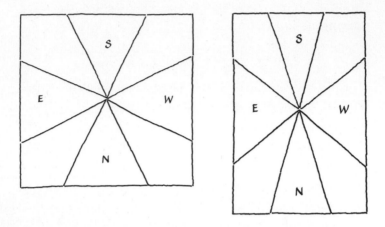

Figure 3G: A square home has better feng shui than a long, thin, rectangular home.

The Lo Shu Magic Square

We can also transfer the trigrams onto a three-by-three magic square. This is the famous Lo Shu square that was found on the shell of a tortoise that came out of the Yellow River about 2205 B.C.E. The nine numbers on this tortoise's shell added up to fifteen in every direction, horizontally, vertically, and diagonally. Fifteen also happens to be the number of days in each of the twenty-four phases of the solar year. This arrangement of numbers was easily incorporated into the pa-kua, with the eight trigrams being placed into position around the center square.

The Lo Shu magic square became one of the cornerstones of Taoism, and its rituals still incorporate the square today. The Lo Shu square is also the famous Square of Saturn, used by the Hebrews. Obviously, mystical knowledge was being exchanged thousands of years ago.

Evaluating Your Own Home

To work out the eight directions in your own home you need an accurately scaled floor plan. If your home is square or oblong in shape you can then draw a three-by-three magic square of the same size to place on top. Alternatively, you may find it easier to simply draw the magic square directly on to your plan.

If your home is an unusual shape, you may have to divide it into a number of sectors and work out the eight directions from the center of each sector (Figure 3H). In fact, you can even do this exercise with a single room if you wish. Bedrooms are commonly assessed in this way to determine the best position for the bed. On the other extreme, you could construct a magic square over a plan of your state or country to determine the best place to live.

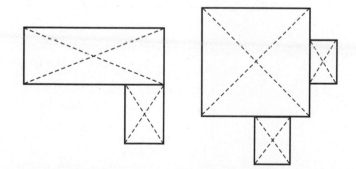

Figure 3H: If your home is an unusual shape, divide it into smaller sections, then evaluate each.

The magic square is constructed with the eight trigrams placed in their respective positions. For instance, if your home faced east and the back sat to the west, you would be living in a Tui home. Your magic square would have east at the bottom of the chart and west at the top (Figure 3I). The sitting directions of the eight trigrams determine their placements in the square. For instance, the top left square in Figure 3I depicts the southwest direction. In Figure 3A we can see that the trigram that sits in that direction is K'un, so consequently, K'un is placed in that particular square.

The completed square is placed over the plan of the home. Let's assume that you live in the Tui home shown in Figure 3E (page 60). We create Figure 3J by superimposing Figure 3I on top of Figure 3E.

Sitting West

K'UN Health	TUI Prime	CHIEN Prosperity
LI 5 ghosts	TUI	K'AN Disaster
SUN 6 Shar	CHEN Death	KEN Longevity

S (left)   N (right)

Facing East

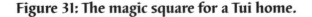

Figure 3I: The magic square for a Tui home.

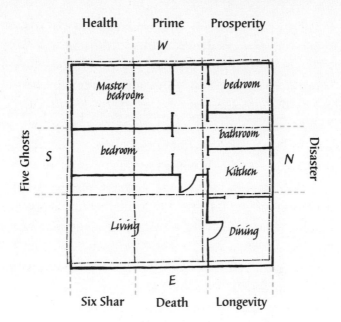

Figure 3J: Superimpose the magic square over the floor plan to evaluate the home.

We can now interpret the chart.

We start by looking for the Prime position, which in this Tui home is in the west. Some of this is wasted as it is part of the hallway, but the rest is in the master bedroom, which is excellent. It promotes peace and harmony. The rest of this bedroom is the Health position, also an excellent position for this room. It promotes health, financial rewards, and good family relationships.

The Prosperity position houses another bedroom, providing a good location and wonderful potential for the person who sleeps here. It could even lead to fame and fortune. However, it also encompasses the bathroom and toilet, which is not a good location.

The final good position is Longevity, and in this home it contains the dining room. This promotes health and harmony at the dining table, making it one of the best possible places for this room. The family will enjoy many pleasant times eating, and simply being together, in this room.

We now start to look at the negative placements. The Death location is at the front door and includes a large part of the living room. This is the area for accidents and misfortune. The rest of the living room is made up by the Six Shar and Five Ghosts, both bad locations. The Six Shar is related to loss, misfortune, rumours, and scandals, and the Five Ghosts are related to theft, fire hazards, and bad influences. Obviously, the living room is in an extremely bad location. The Five Ghosts also includes the third bedroom, and is a bad site for this room.

Finally, we look at the kitchen. This is sited in the Disaster location, which signifies anger, quarrels, disputes, and the potential for fire. Definitely not a harmonious working environment!

Again, every home has four good and four bad locations, of course. Only occasionally will you find a home that has every room sited at the correct location.

Fortunately, there are many things we can do to improve the feng shui of these bad rooms and make them harmonious and more pleasant places to live. These will be covered later.

The Aspirations of the Pa-Kua

In addition to determining positive and negative directions the pa-kua can also be used to find the aspirations that we all have. Most people want to be rich, happy, successful and appreciated. We also want to love and be loved in return. The aspirations of the pa-kua represent all of these things (Figure 3K).

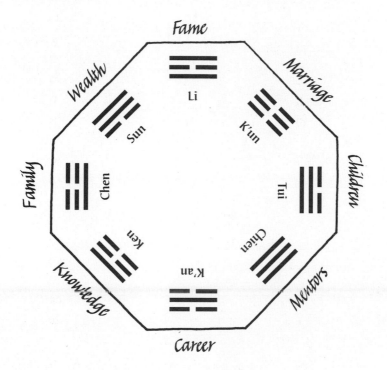

Figure 3K: The aspirations of the pa-kua.

Chen represents the health and well-being of loved ones. The keyword is "family."

Sun represents money and financial matters. The keyword is "wealth."

Li represents reputation and standing in the community. The keyword is "fame."

K'un represents love and other emotional relationships. The keyword is "marriage."

Tui represents children and other direct descendants. The keyword is "children."

Chien represents people who are helpful to us, including teachers and others who have given us valuable assistance and advice. The keyword is "mentors."

K'an represents work and other opportunities for growth. The keyword is "career."

Ken represents study and learning. The keyword is "knowledge."

The aspirations of the pa-kua are controversial for a number of reasons. First, the compass directions are ignored completely. This is the main reason why many feng shui practitioners to not use the aspirations. What is the point, they say, of having a Compass School when the compass points are not used? Consequently, the aspirations are used more by adherents to the Form School than practitioners of the Compass School. The whole matter is complicated further by the fact that most professional feng shui practitioners use both schools in making their assessments.

Another reason the aspirations are controversial is that the results can sometimes disagree with the positive and negative directions of the pa-kua. This means that people may find that a room is perfect using the directions of the pa-kua, but is completely wrong when using the aspirations. An example would be if the toilet was in the Death, Disaster, Six Shar, or Five Ghosts locations. These are all good positions for the placement of the toilet. However, the aspirations may place Sun in that position. Sun represents money. This means that all the money in the household would be wasted away (go down the toilet, in effect).

Actually, the situation is not nearly as bad as that. The positive and negative directions relate largely to what is going on inside the home. The aspirations start inside the home, but spread outwards and away, so have most effect outside the home. Consequently, in the example above, the Six Shar direction is a good place for the toilet, but that direction could also be a good place for Sun to be as the occupants of the home could well find money in that direction.

I have included the controversial aspirations in this book for the sake of completeness. In practice, both the aspirations and the pa-kua directions have a part to play, but I pay much more attention to the positive and negative directions than I do to the aspirations.

Finding the Aspirations

When finding the aspirations, the pa-kua is placed in position with K'an parallel to the front door. (For this method, we totally ignore the compass directions.) Once this is done, you will see which parts of your home represent different aspirations. You may find, for instance, that Sun, representing prosperity, is in the bathroom and all your wealth is going down the toilet. You may also find that K'un, representing marriage, is in the master bedroom, indicating great happiness in this area of your life.

Here is an example of the aspirations placed over the same Tui home used in previous examples (Figure 3E, page 60). In Figure 3L, we see that the front door faces the east, so this section must contain K'an. K'an represents work and career, and in this home is found in the living room. This room would not be a restful place for the inhabitants and much of the conversation would revolve around their careers. The east would be a good direction for the inhabitants to find work and a career.

In the southeast direction we have Ken, which represents study and learning. In this home Ken is also in the living room, not usually the best place in the home for quiet study. The southeast direction would be a good place for people living here to attend school, college, or other centers of learning.

In the south we find Chen. Chen relates to family matters and in this home is well-sited as it covers one bedroom and a small part of the master bedroom. Happy times as a family could be found in a southern direction.

In the southwest we have Sun in the master bedroom. Sun relates to financial concerns. This could work well, in some respects, but there would be an undue emphasis on money matters in this room. However, the southwest would be the best direction for investments and other money-making opportunities.

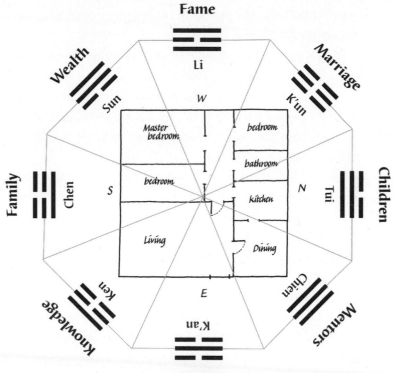

Figure 3L: To find the aspirations, place the pa-kua with K'an parallel to the front door.

In the west we have Li, which represents fame and standing in the community. Unfortunately, half of this is dissipated in the hallway, though the master bedroom benefits from its influence. If the occupants wish to raise their standing in the community, they should look for opportunities to do so in the west.

In the northwest we have K'un which represents love and romance. In this home a bedroom benefits from its influence. This could be either good or bad, depending on the age of the people who sleep in this room. Any occupant of the home who wanted to find love and romance would be likely to find it in this direction.

Tui, representing children, is in the north. This area includes the kitchen and part of a bedroom. Quite a bit of work involving children will take place in the kitchen. This means much more than preparing meals. In this home the children will do most of their confiding to their parents in the kitchen. The children of the home would find most of their happiest times would be spent in a northern direction.

Finally, we have the northeast direction. In this position we have Chien, which represents people who are helpful to us. This is well-sited as the dining room takes up most of Chien's space. This would be the best room in the home to entertain and obtain guidance from people who have our best interests at heart. Also, the occupants would be likely to find a good friend or mentor in the northeast.

We do not normally compare the aspirations with the fortunate and unfortunate locations, as they represent different things. The locations always refer to what is inside the walls of the home, but with the aspirations the influence of the direction can continue indefinitely.

Fortunately, there are remedies that can remove the negative aspects of any bad locations in your home. For instance, flower arrangements and potted plants can improve family relationships and marriage when placed in these areas of the home. A large statue placed in the Career sector will ensure a more successful, stable future career. We will cover remedies in more depth in Chapter 6.

4

The Flying Star

There are several systems of feng shui, but the best known are the Form School and the Compass School systems. They evolved separately, but by the end of the nineteenth century most feng shui practitioners were using both methods.[1]

The Flying Star system enables us to look into the future and see what the feng shui influences on us will be. It is a branch of the Compass School that deals with future trends, and evolved directly from the giant tortoise that Wu found in the River Lo some five thousand years ago. Contained in the markings of this tortoise's shell was a pattern (Figure 4A, next page) that the ancients discovered made up a perfect three-by-three magic square. Each horizontal, vertical, and diagonal column added up to fifteen. This square is known as the Lo Shu (Figure 4B, next page).

This find was so remarkable that the ancient scholars analyzed it in great depth, trying to understand the meaning behind it. The result of their research created not only the Flying Star system of feng shui, but also Chinese astrology, numerology, the Nine Star Ki, and the I Ching.

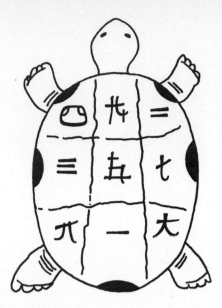

Figure 4A: The markings on a tortoise shell were a pattern for a perfect three-by-three magic square.

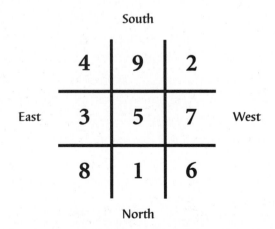

Figure 4B: The Lo Shu.

Each number represents a direction. North is always placed at the bottom of the diagram, making the chart appear to be upside down. Consequently, the number one indicates north, two indicates southwest, three indicates east, and so on. These directions are of great importance in feng shui.[2]

Each number was also given a meaning, and these are used for predicting future events.

One (water) is considered a good number.

Two (earth) is one of two unlucky numbers and represents ill health.

Three (wood) relates to anger, stress, disputes, and conflicts.

Four (wood) relates to love, sex, and education.

Five (earth) is the other unlucky number. It represents oppression and misfortune.

Six (metal) is a good number that represents prosperity in the past because it also represents the years 1964 to 1983.

Seven (metal) relates to communication, entertainment, and spiritual matters. It indicates current prosperity because it also represents the years 1983 to 2003.

Eight (earth) is the best number, indicating good fortune and prosperity in the near future.

Nine (fire) represents good luck and future prosperity.

These meanings have no relation to standard numerological interpretations. Interestingly enough, these definitions sometimes surprise modern-day Chinese people. For instance, they tend to avoid the number four as the Cantonese word for four sounds like *death*. Likewise, two, an unlucky number in feng shui, sounds like *easy* in Cantonese. However, eight sounds like *prosperity* in Cantonese, which accords perfectly with its feng shui meaning.

The numbers two and eight are referred to as shars as the word *shar* sounds like the Mandarin word for *kill*. Shars are negative energies that can be created in a variety of ways. Feng shui has many ways of reducing the impact of shars, but you must first be aware of them before you can do anything about them.

The position of the planet Jupiter also creates a shar known as the Grand Duke. Jupiter was considered so powerful that all of the Chinese years are named after the position of this planet.

- In the Year of the Rat, Jupiter is directly north.
- In the Year of the Ox, Jupiter is northeast.
- In the Year of the Tiger, Jupiter is northeast.
- In the Year of the Rabbit, Jupiter is east.
- In the Year of the Dragon, Jupiter is southeast.
- In the Year of the Snake, Jupiter is southeast.
- In the Year of the Horse, Jupiter is south.
- In the Year of the Ram, Jupiter is southwest.
- In the Year of the Monkey, Jupiter is southwest.
- In the Year of the Rooster, Jupiter is west.
- In the Year of the Dog, Jupiter is northwest.
- In the Year of the Pig, Jupiter is northwest.

The ancient Chinese warlords always avoided advancing in the direction of Jupiter, preferring to keep it behind their back. Even today, it is still believed that facing the Grand Duke (Jupiter), or sitting in a position opposite him will bring bad luck.

The position that conflicts with the Grand Duke is known as Three Shars, and naturally, this area is also avoided if at all possible. People in the Three Shars position who are facing the Grand Duke feel like they could be stabbed in the back. Office workers try to avoid working in this position as it is believed that it will tempt fate and lead to much bad luck and misfortune. Builders and developers also avoid working in this position, as it is believed that they will be interfering with the earth above the duke's head.[3]

In the years of the dog, horse, and tiger, the Three Shars position is in the north. In the years of the ox, rooster, and snake, the Three Shars position is in the east. In the years of the boar, rabbit, and sheep, the Three Shars position is in the West.

The numbers are not fixed in position, and their movements reveal the pattern of the feng shui forces. Figure 4B shows the standard Lo Shu diagram, which is also known as the "universal table."

We are currently in the Seven Period (from 1984 to 2003), which means we need to have the number seven in the central position in the magic square. To do this, we add two to each number in the Lo Shu diagram. Number nine is followed by a one, so the number placed in the south position of the Seven Period square is a two, and the number placed in the northeast position is a one (8 + 2 = 9 + 1). This chart is shown on the next page as Figure 4C.

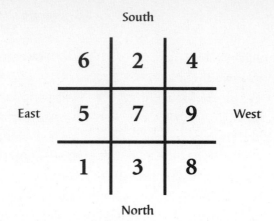

South

6	2	4
5	7	9
1	3	8

East   West

North

Figure 4C: The Period of Seven (1984–2003).

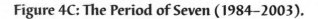

9	5	7
8	1	3
4	6	2

1	6	8
9	2	4
5	7	3

2	7	9
1	3	5
6	8	4

3	8	1
2	4	6
7	9	5

4	9	2
3	5	7
8	1	6

5	1	3
4	6	8
9	2	7

6	2	4
5	7	9
1	3	8

7	3	5
6	8	1
2	4	9

8	4	6
7	9	2
3	5	1

Figure 4D: Pattern of movement.

The nine possible combinations are also shown in Figure 4D. These squares can also be used for every year, month, and day. All we need do is ensure that the reigning number is in the center. Note that these numbers go in descending order. If the reigning (central) number for January happens to be a six, the number in the center of the February chart would be a five, and March would be a four.

We can superimpose these charts on top of each other to determine the likely events that could occur during any period of time. We already know that we are in a Seven Period. This chart (Figure 4C) has an effect on every house built between 1984 and 2003.

Let's say that we would like to know what conditions will be like in our house in July 1999. First of all we draw up a chart for the year 1999. This chart has a one in the center position (Figure 4D). This is determined from the table "Central Position Numbers for Years 1901 to 2017" on page 168 of the Appendix. We now draw up a chart for July 1999 (this has a seven in the central position).

The monthly number is determined by the year number shown on the left side of the table "Central Position Numbers for the Months of the Year" on page 167 of the Appendix. In the 1, 4, and 7 years, January is a 4 month, February is a 3 month, March is a 2, April a 1, May a 9, June an 8, July a 7, August a 6, September a 5, October a 4, November a 3, and December a 2. In the 2, 5, and 8, years, January is a 1, February a 9, March an 8, and so on. In the 3, 6, and 9 years, January is a 7, February a 6, and so on.

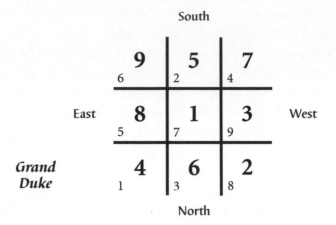

Figure 4E: July 1999.

Finally, we superimpose the monthly chart on to the yearly one (Figure 4E). The monthly chart is represented by the small numbers.

When we look at the chart we immediately see that the numbers two and five, the two worst numbers, are together in the south position. This is a particularly bad shar. It means that something unpleasant could happen to someone who lived in that particular room of the house in July, unless, of course, there were other good feng shui influences to counteract it. One remedy would be to hang metal wind chimes in a southerly position. The metallic sound of the wind chimes would counteract and weaken the earth energy coming from the five. Six coins hung on a string would also help reduce the effect of the two. They should also be hung in a southerly position while the number two is in the south square.

The east room has an eight influence for the year, indicating money in the near future. July, though, would be the opposite because of the monthly influence of the five. The person who lived in this room would have to take particular care with money matters in this month.

Let's take another example. The chart for March 1997 is shown below in Figure 4F. (The monthly chart is again represented by the small numbers.) This house has numbers one, six, and eight situated in the east, northeast, and north positions. These are all favorable. In March the one and eight are both doubled, creating an especially favorable month for people living in these rooms.

It is a good idea to check out the feng shui of your home at least once a year as the energies are constantly changing. Probably the best time is in February when the new lunar year starts and the shars change position.

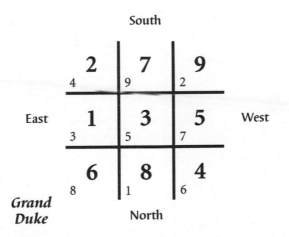

Figure 4F: March 1997.

We can take all of this further by superimposing the yearly and monthly charts on top of the chart for the Seven Period (1984–2003). The table "Central Position Numbers for Years 1901 to 2017" in the Appendix (page 168) shows the numbers in the center of every year chart for a one-hundred-year period.

Look at the effect on someone living in the south room in July 1999 when the month and year are placed on top of the Seven Period chart (Figure 4G). For that month, the south room consists of two twos and a five. This creates a very serious shar.

Let's look at another example. Since this house was built in 1990 we use the same Seven Period chart. Let's look at this house in September 1995 (Figure 4H). The plan of the house is shown in Figure 4I. The front door is in the southwest

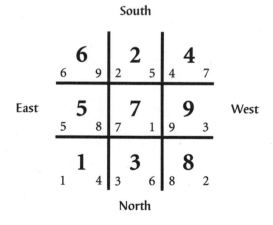

Figure 4G: The charts for the year 1999 and the month of July are placed over the chart for the Seven Period.

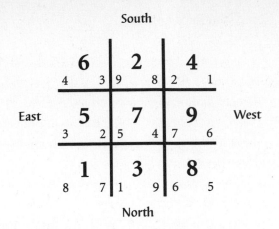

South

6 4 3	2 9 8	4 2 1
5 3 2	7 5 4	9 7 6
1 8 7	3 1 9	8 6 5

East · · · West

North

Figure 4H: The charts for the year 1995 and the month of September are placed over the chart for the Seven Period.

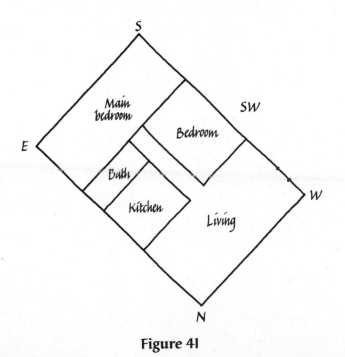

Figure 4I

position and the main bedroom is in the southeast. In September, the southwest square contained a two, the central square a five, and the east square a two and a five. This indicates very bad energy entering the house and affecting the people who use the east bedroom. The likelihood of accident and/or illness was extremely high.

Assume that the same house was built in another direction, with the front door facing west (Figure 4J). This also created a bad shar in September 1995, as the northwest square contained a five, the central square a five, and the south square a two. In this case, the ill effects would not be quite as bad because there is only one negative number in each square.

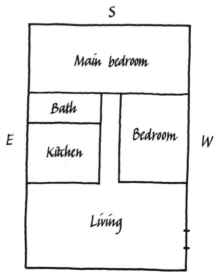

Figure 4J

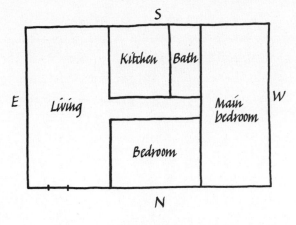

Figure 4K

Finally, assume that the house was built facing north (Figure 4K). In this instance, the northeast square contained an eight, one, and seven, all good numbers. The central square contained a five, seven, and four, and the bedroom (now in the west position) contained a nine, seven, and six. Seven is regarded as being a lucky, fortunate number in the Period of Seven, and each of these squares contained this number. Consequently, the occupants of this bedroom would have had an extremely fortunate, happy, and financially successful month.

5

The Luo-Pan

The Chinese were the inventors of the compass, and it appears that they invented it twice.

The legend is that Emperor Shih Huang Ti fought a battle against Prince Ch'ih Yu about 206 B.C.E. The prince was given a special, magical mist by his sorcerers that prevented the emperor's men from being able to see his approaching army.

Fortunately for the emperor's army, a magical chariot appeared. A lifelike human figure was mounted on it, with an outstretched arm that always pointed towards the south. This was the direction the prince's army was approaching from, so the emperor's troops were able to follow the chariot to victory. The legend claims that the chariot was magnetic.

This story sounds like many others where some sort of divine or magical help saved a difficult situation. However, some years ago some three hundred ancient compasses were excavated in China,[1] proving that compasses were in fact known at this time. The compasses that were found are known as the Sinan compasses. They are made in two parts. The base is a metal plate, some four inches square. Engraved in the middle of this is a small circle, about three and a quarter inches in diameter, surrounded by the eight trigrams. The other section is a metal spoon an inch and a half long. The bowl of the spoon is placed in the center of the circle on the base plate. Because the spoon is magnetic, it spins and stops with the handle pointing towards the south and the bowl towards the north. In China compasses have always indicated south, rather than north. This is because the soil and climate is better in the south, and consequently this direction was always considered the better place in which to live.

It is believed that the Sinan compass was used during the Western Han Dynasty (206 B.C.E.–24 C.E.). It seems strange that something as useful as a compass was forgotten for more than a thousand years. Probably, the Sinan compass was used by a Taoist sect who kept it secret and used it for their own purposes. It wasn't until some 1,300 years later that the first documented use of the compass was recorded in the eleventh century C.E. By the twelfth century, knowledge of the compass was well known and it was being used in Arabia and Europe.

The Compass School of feng shui began about this time, and the **luo-pan**, the Chinese geomancer's compass, was devised. *Luo* means *reticulated* and *pan* means *dish*. "Reticulated dish" is a good description as the luo-pan looks a little bit like a spider's web.

A luo-pan is usually square in shape and looks extremely complicated. The square base is divided into quarters by two lengths of red thread, which act as cross hairs. A compass is in the middle, surrounded by a number of circles containing important information related to geology and astronomy. The number of circles varies according to the complexity of the luo-pan. Some simple ones have just six circles of information; others have up to thirty-six. The one I use is a compromise, and contains thirteen circles. These circles are known as *Tseng*, meaning *stories* or *layers*.

The compass is in the center, and is known as the "Pool of Heaven." This is probably because early compass needles floated on a small drop of water. The needle of the compass indicates south. A fine line bisects the circle containing the needle. This acts as a guide line.

Around this, the first ring contains the eight trigrams indicating the eight directions (north, northeast, east, southeast, south, southwest, west, northwest). The trigrams can be found in either the Former Heaven or Latter Heaven sequences. Most luo-pans that I have seen have been arranged in the Latter Heaven sequence. Sometimes, this first circle contains the numbers of the Lo Shu magic square relating to the eight trigrams. The second ring contains the five elements and eight of the Ten Heavenly Stems (of Chinese astrology). Around this is a ring containing twenty-four points, including the twelve earthly branches (again from Chinese astrology).

The different rings vary from this point on, depending on the complexity of the luo-pan. The eighth circle is a useful one, as it is in effect a calendar telling you when and where you should erect a house, temple, or tomb.[2] One of the outer circles divides the circle into 360 degrees. Some of these are marked in red, denoting lucky positions. Others, marked in black, are unlucky, and the rest are neutral. An experienced feng shui master can obtain a wealth of material from his or her luo-pan. The feng shui practitioner would start by using the luo-pan to determine the facing and sitting positions of the building. He or she would then refer to the information in the different rings of the luo-pan to help decide what can be done to improve the feng shui of the structure.

Naturally, the writing on luo-pans is in Chinese, but English language luo-pans are now available.[3] A good quality compass will also work just as well in determining directions, but, if you become really involved in the subject you will ultimately want your own luo-pan.

Using the Luo-Pan

Your luo-pan should always be stored in a horizontal position. It should be treated carefully to avoid any damage that would affect its accuracy. For instance, it should never be left in a parked car.

To use the luo-pan, start by removing your watch and any heavy jewelry that might distort the readings of the compass.

Determine the facing direction of the building. Stand either just inside or outside the entrance and hold the luo-pan at waist height. Make sure that you are well away from anything metallic, such as a parked car or an iron beam. Wait until the needle stops moving. Rotate the compass dial until the needle is aligned with the guide line bisecting the Pool of Heaven that contains the needle.

The vertical crosshair will now indicate the facing and sitting directions of the building. Much more information can be gained by checking the signs under the red cross-hair threads. For instance, the feng shui practitioner can quickly determine the compatibility of the householder's personal trigram with that of the trigram relating to the sitting position of the building.

Confirm your reading by doing it three more times from different positions. One position is about ten feet forward from where you took the initial reading, and the other two are on each side of the original position.

Another, probably more accurate, method of using the luo-pan is to align one edge of it with the facing wall. Again, the results should be confirmed by additional readings in case the wall is not perfectly straight. This is the method used to check the positions of yin houses (graves). One side of the luo-pan is put in contact with the facing direction of the grave, and then the usual procedure is followed.

6

Shar Remedies

Shars, or negative ch'i, are caused by a wide variety of occurrences, and we have already covered most of these. Remedies are often very simple. Erecting a fence or hedge to eliminate a shar coming from the house across the road is a simple solution. Once the shar is hidden from view, it can no longer exert a harmful effect. Erecting a mirror, enclosed in a pa-kua, on the fence will also reflect the shar away. Blocking off a door to eliminate having three doors in a row is a more complicated type of solution.

Friends of mine were once suffering an extended run of bad luck. I found it hard to believe the change in their house when I went to visit them. As their fortunes declined they had become less and less motivated to do any work on their property. As a result, the front garden had become over-grown until it was taller than the house, and their home could not even be seen from the road. This blocked the beneficial ch'i and stopped it from entering the house. They thought I was crazy to suggest chopping it all back, but their fortunes started to improve just as soon as they had done it.

In practice, there are a number of remedies that can be used. Bright lights are very beneficial. They eliminate any dark spots in the house, and cast a cheerful glow on the room. They are especially good for stimulating areas of your home that you want to boost. The entrance to your home should always appear warm and welcoming, and bright lights can help this. You may want to boost the fame area of your house (based on the aspirations of the pa-kua super-imposed over your home). Increasing the amount of light in this area of your house will help your progress immeasur-ably. Lights can also serve to balance irregularly shaped rooms. By placing a light in the area that is out of shape you can eliminate the negative effects.

Any form of lighting helps, but crystal chandeliers can be extremely powerful. Not only is the light beneficial, but the crystals also add strength by reflecting the light in different directions, magnifying the good ch'i. If a chandelier is not suitable for the location, use a brightly colored shade that is in harmony with your element.

Any object made of crystal is beneficial. Crystal vases, bowls, paperweights, and ornaments all help create an abundance of ch'i. Crystals can act as prisms, breaking down the sun's rays and creating colorful rainbows. This brings good luck as well as good ch'i, and many Chinese people suspend prisms and crystals in positions where the sun can shine on them. Crystals can also avert the negative ch'i created from three doors in a row. Simply suspend a crystal in one of the doorways.

Mirrors are arguably the most useful device for deflecting potential shars. Place them anywhere to deflect problems.

The angle of the roof on the house across the road, an unsightly drain, a straight road, a flyover, and a building that dwarfs yours can all be deflected by the judicious use of a mirror. If your bed is not able to face the door for some reason, a mirror in the right position will enable you to see people as they enter the room. Likewise, the cook should also work in such a position that he or she can see anyone who comes in the door of the kitchen. A strategically placed mirror allows him or her to see the door.

Mirrors reflect light into areas that would otherwise be too dark. This attracts ch'i into the area as well. Mirrors can also reflect into the house attractive views of the exterior. This is particularly favorable if the outside view is of rolling countryside, or a stream or lake.

Mirrors can be any size, but generally speaking, the larger the better. Floor to ceiling mirrors are favored as they do not appear to cut off people's heads or feet. The exception to this is mirrors surrounded by a pa-kua. With these, the mirror gains strength from the trigrams placed around it.

A pa-kua mirror is also known as a yang mirror. As you know, yang is active, so the pa-kua mirror actively protects and guards the house from negative energies. Ordinary mirrors are known as yin mirrors. They are passive and attract beneficial ch'i.

Be very careful with mirror tiles. Because they distort reflections, they can create negative ch'i.

You cannot have too many mirrors in your home. In the dining room they appear to double the amount of food available, creating feelings of wealth and prosperity. They can also expand the size of small rooms, and correct the appearance of rooms that are irregular in shape.

Live animals, such as goldfish, are also very useful in eliminating shars and creating beneficial ch'i. Water is a symbol of wealth. In Cantonese, the word *sui* means both water and money. Many Asian business people have paintings of water scenes in their offices, because the picture symbolizes water flowing in. This carries on to include animals that live in the water, such as fish. Aquariums are extremely common in the Orient. They symbolize wealth for people who do not have a water view. Whenever possible, they contain nine goldfish. Eight of these are gold, representing money and financial success, while the other one is black to symbolize protection. (However, if you live in an area plagued with petty burglaries, it is better to have eight black fish and one red. This is because the black fish help protect you from petty crime. Goldfish, on the other hand, increase your wealth and luck.)[1]

It is a commonly held belief that any bad luck that enters the home is attracted to the fish and absorbed by them. When a fish dies, especially the black one, it is a sign that some bad luck has been averted.

A famous Chinese story concerns carp that swim upstream. When they reach the "Golden Gates" they jump over and become transformed into celestial dragons. This used to be related to passing the Official examinations and starting a successful career working for the emperor.[2] Consequently, fish are also seen as symbolizing success in both examinations and career.

Tortoises have always been a symbol of good luck, because, as you know, the original magic square (Lo Shu) was found on the back of a tortoise by Wu of Hsia. Tortoises also symbolize wisdom, stability, and longevity.

The island of Penang, in Malaysia, is sometimes referred to as the "Isle of the Upturned Tortoise" as its shape looks just like a tortoise lying on its back.[3] It is popular with tourists as the pace is slow and casual. It is also a popular place for pensioners who choose it partly because of the longevity promised by its shape, but also because they find it such a relaxing place to spend their final years.

Interestingly enough, ornaments depicting goldfish and tortoises can also produce the same beneficial effect as the actual animals and are popular in many homes.

Bats are an unusual animal in feng shui. They are not used very often as most people do not realize their significance. In feng shui they are considered to be highly intelligent animals who see the world from quite a different perspective as they hang upside-down.

Butterflies are believed to contain the souls of people who have recently died. They symbolize joy, happiness, and eternal life.

The crane creates a graceful symbol of purity, honesty, and justice. It is also considered a symbol of longevity. In ancient China magistrates and judges had paintings and ornaments of cranes in their chambers, hence the association with justice.

The phoenix is a common theme in Chinese paintings. This mythical bird, which can burn, then rise again from its ashes, is a potent symbol of rebirth. It symbolizes peace, harmony, and self-sacrifice.

Paintings of fierce animals are often used to protect the home. Usually, these are of birds of prey, such as the eagle. Paintings such as these should be kept outside the front door, because if kept inside they could turn against the occupants. Outside, they are believed to protect the home from harm.

Small statues of lions, tigers, and bears are kept inside the house to act as symbolic protective talismans. Replicas of stone temple lions can be bought in many novelty stores.

Plants also create ch'i and excellent feng shui, as they symbolize life and growth. The plants have to be healthy, though; sickly looking plants are a sign of bad ch'i. Consequently, if your plants are rotting or dying, you need to attend to them right away. Replace them, if necessary, with healthier plants. Dying plants symbolize death. Healthy plants symbolize life, growth, and abundance. They are especially beneficial when placed at the entrance as they encourage ch'i and prosperity into the building. Plants are also an effective way to conceal and block off poison arrows. They can conceal sharp corners created by walls or furniture. Pillars and columns can create bad shars if they are square in shape. Mirrors and plants can eliminate the harmful effects of these.

Bamboo is a very popular plant in feng shui as it is believed to possess strange powers that repel negative elements. It is also evergreen, and is considered a symbol of longevity and endurance.

Cut flowers brighten up the appearance of rooms and create good ch'i, especially if they are colorful. This is another good reason to send plants or flowers to a sick friend.

There are five flowers that are especially beneficial for feng shui purposes. The most important of these is the peony, which is considered to represent wealth and honor. It also symbolizes love and, when it flowers, great fortune.

The chrysanthemum represents happiness and laughter. It is frequently displayed in the home as it symbolizes a life of comfort and ease. Both peonies and chrysanthemums are seen everywhere during the Chinese New Year celebrations.

White magnolias and orchids symbolize sweetness, good taste, and femininity.

The lotus is regarded as a sacred flower by Buddhists. It symbolizes purity, not surprisingly, as it rises from muddy water and lies on the surface, triumphant and gorgeous. Displayed in the home, it represents peace, tranquility, creativity, and spiritual growth.

Imitation plants and flowers achieve the same effect. Nowadays, you can buy beautiful artificial silk and paper flowers that look exactly like the real thing. However, they must be looked after. An imitation plant that is allowed to gather dust will create bad ch'i. If it is looked after, it will create an abundance of good ch'i. Dried flowers are the only exception and should be avoided. Because they have dried up from a lack of water, they are extremely bad feng shui.

Flowers can be placed in various parts of the house to stimulate the areas you want to revitalize in your life. Flowers belong to the wood element and are very beneficial for people born in a fire element year (as wood creates fire).

The east (family) and southeast (wealth) sectors of the home represent wood, and flowers placed here will improve family relationships and help create prosperity. The fire sector (south) also benefits from flowers, and this will increase your good name and standing in the community. The southwest sector relates to marriage and flowers here can do a great deal to revive and reactivate permanent relationships. Place flowers in the north sector of your home if you wish to make more progress in your career.

Trees and plants are especially beneficial if you were born in a fire or wood element year. If you were born in an earth or water year, though, you should be careful not to surround yourself with too many plants. This is because wood destroys earth and drains water. Simply use common sense and use plants and flowers as feng shui aids, but do not overdo it.

Fruits can also be used to avert shars and create beneficial ch'i. The peach is the most important of these. It symbolizes marriage and eternal life. It is often called the "fruit of the immortal," and can often be seen in paintings of the Chinese immortals.

Oranges symbolize wealth, happiness, and abundance. At the time of the Chinese New Year they are displayed in the home, eaten, and given as gifts. The Chinese word for orange is *kum*, which sounds like *gold*.

Wind chimes are very popular as feng shui remedies. They are usually made from metal, bamboo or other woods, and glass or crystal. They make a cheerful, tinkling sound when blown by a breeze or gust of air. They should ideally consist of either five or eight tubes around a center piece.

For feng shui purposes the tubes must be hollow. Avoid wind chimes made with solid rods. Hollow wind chimes, such as bamboo rods, allow the ch'i to rise upwards bringing happiness and good luck to the household.

Wind chimes are very effective at removing bad ch'i, and can be placed anywhere where they will pick up movement of air. The tinkling sounds symbolize the movement of beneficial ch'i.

Metal wind chimes are highly beneficial when placed in either the west or northwest sectors of your home, as these are the metal areas. The west also represents children, so metal wind chimes in this location will help provide you with children, if that is what you want. The northwest governs mentors, and a metal wind chime here will attract such people to you. Metal also activates the north (water) sector, which governs your career. Wind chimes placed here will help you advance in your chosen profession.

Bamboo, or other types of wooden wind chimes work best in the east (family) and southeast (wealth) sectors of your home. Wooden wind chimes placed here will help your family life and prosperity. (One word of warning: never place metal wind chimes in the east or southeast sectors of your home. This is because metal overpowers and destroys wood.) This south sector of your home influences your standing in the community, and bamboo wind chimes here can help you improve your status and maybe even achieve fame.

Other cylindrical, hollow objects, such as flutes, create beneficial ch'i. When played by a skilled flautist, a flute stimulates and energizes ch'i, creating contentment and a sense of well-being for the occupants of the house.

Some feng shui practitioners insist that wind chimes must be hung out of doors. Others have no objection to them being placed indoors. I can vouch for the beneficial effects of having a wind chime indoors in a long corridor. Mobiles can take the place of wind chimes indoors, if desired, and this makes a satisfactory compromise for people who are concerned about any negative effects from having wind chimes inside the house.

We have already discussed the beneficial effects of water. Fountains create especially strong ch'i and are related to wealth and prosperity. Fountains used to be found mainly out of doors in parks and entrances to public buildings. Nowadays, it is not uncommon to find them inside people's homes. They are pleasing to look at, and symbolize wealth and successful financial dealings.[4]

Naturally, the very best position for a fountain inside your home is in the wealth (southeast) sector. Small fountains that recycle the water are not expensive. Buy one that is pleasant-looking and watch your fortunes increase.

Your career can be enhanced by placing an aquarium, or something else containing water, in the north sector of your home. This is particularly beneficial for people born in a wood or water element year. You can improve your home and family life by placing water in the east sector of your home. Your fortunes will improve if you place an aquarium in the wealth (southeast) sector. If you are seeking fame, place an aquarium in the south sector.

Large objects can bring strength and confidence into the home, increasing the flow of beneficial ch'i. Large rocks, sculptures, and statues create yang energy and can effectively balance areas that contain too much yin.

In the East, statues are very popular for this purpose. Statues of Buddha are the ones most easily recognized in the West. There are several different types of statues of Buddha. The most popular of these is the Maitreya Buddha, often known as the Laughing Buddha. He is depicted with a smiling face and a large pot belly (which is believed to contain great wealth). Chinese people believe that if you stroke his stomach once every day you will attract good luck. Statues of Buddha should be displayed so that the statue looks down on the occupants of the house, rather than the other way around.

In Chinese homes the most popular statues are of the three Star Gods. In fact, it would be hard to find a Chinese home that did not contain these important symbols of good fortune. These are the gods of happiness (*Fu'k*), affluence (*Lu'k*), and longevity (*Sau*).

There are also several gods of wealth and a number of goddesses. By far the most popular goddess is Kuan Yin, the goddess of mercy. She is also found in most Chinese households and is believed to answer prayers and help people who need her.

The correct use of color can also avert shars and create beneficial ch'i. The right colors for you are derived from the five elements (see Chapter 1). The right color for one person might be totally wrong for someone else.

The main exception to this is red, which has always been regarded as the color of good fortune, happiness, and prosperity. This explains why red is such a popular color in the

East. Chinese brides dress in scarlet to symbolize blessings from heaven, and a long, stable, successful marriage. Red packets (containing money) are given to children and employees during the Chinese New Year. Red revitalizes, and is a good color for people who are lazy or lacking in energy. The precious stone associated with red is ruby. However, red should not be used on doors, gates, or walls that face east or west, as it is believed to create negative ch'i in these positions.

Gold and green are also considered fortunate colors. Gold, of course, symbolizes the sun and the metal, and attracts success and a good reputation. Green symbolizes spring, the time of rebirth and new growth. Green is a restful, tranquil color. The precious stone is emerald.

Yellow is associated with learning and the development of intuition. It is related to ambition and ultimate wisdom. Gold is the precious element associated with yellow.

Blue symbolizes thoughtfulness and consideration for others. Sapphire is the precious stone associated with blue.

Violet is the color of the visionary and relates to truth and spiritual growth. The precious stone associated with violet is the amethyst.

White is considered to be a pure, neutral color. Yet, when passed through a prism it reveals every other color. It relates to purity and innocence, which is why brides so often wear white. The precious stone related to white is the diamond.

Black is the color of the night, and also of death. It relates to deception, dishonesty, and slander. Black and red should both be used with caution. Black should not be used on doors, gates, fences, or walls that face north or south.

Finally, and possibly surprisingly, radios and television sets can create good ch'i and eliminate shars. This is because these items can create color, sound, and life, all of which stimulate ch'i. Experiment by placing your television in different parts of your house and seeing how it activates the different pa-kua aspiration areas.

Any item that uses electricity is using the universal vibrations that create and aid the flow of beneficial ch'i.

7

Feng Shui for Success

Everyone wants to be successful in his or her chosen career. Novels about wealth and power sell well, allowing us all to vicariously experience the joys of being rich and influential. Not everyone wants to become a millionaire, but we all want to be a little bit more successful than we already are.

With feng shui we can increase the odds in our favor, and use it to generate much more success and happiness in every part of our lives. Good feng shui makes it much easier to live and work in harmony with everyone else. This makes your career path that much smoother.

We begin by evaluating our environment using the Form School. Look for the green dragon and the white tiger both at home and at work. If your home environment is not conducive to good ch'i, move house if at all possible. Otherwise, use the relevant feng shui remedies. Once you have examined your environment thoroughly, begin a more serious examination of the interior of your home.

Start by checking the directions of the main doors in your home: the front door, bedroom door, and office or study door. Lay a pa-kua symbol over a plan of your house and see if these important doors are facing positive directions. It may seem hard to believe that changing the placement of a door could make any difference, but there are many documented instances where it has helped enormously. For instance, in Hong Kong many banks have their entrance doors at an angle to the front of the building. This circumvents the problem of the bank facing an inauspicious direction.

Next, look at the bedroom. Hopefully, your bedroom is square or oblong in shape. If not, you will have to apply some of the feng shui remedies we have already covered.

Ensure that your bedroom is well lit when you are not sleeping. Do not have the curtains closed during the day. Allow as much light and fresh air to enter the room as possible. This is particularly important if you do any reading or studying in the bedroom, because the light attracts good ch'i into the room.

Place a pa-kua over a plan of your bedroom to determine the best locations for your bed. If you want success, you will choose the wealth, fame, and career directions as indicated by the pa-kua aspirations. Naturally, these are not the best positions to choose if you are seeking to start a family, but are the best locations for career and financial success. It may not be possible to place your bed in this location. If it is not practical, see if you can at least lie with your head pointing in the correct direction. This will allow the correct ch'i energy to flow into you while you sleep.

There are two extremely negative positions where you must not place your bed. Do not sleep with your head pointing towards the door. If your bed is aligned on the same wall as the door, do not sleep with your back facing the wall. In feng shui, the best positions are where you can see anyone coming into the room.

You can also activate the best directions in your bedroom with suitable feng shui aids. A pa-kua, mirror, wind chimes, or a crystal can help you get the most help from this area.

The placement of your dressing table is also important. This is the direction you face when you are getting ready to go to work. Make sure that you are facing one of the success directions. Most dressing tables also have a mirror. As you know, this magnifies the ch'i energy, but also enables you to look at yourself while facing a propitious direction.

Finally, while looking at your home make sure that your toilet is not situated in the K'an, or career, sector of your house. This is the worst possible location for your toilet as it literally means that your career potential is being flushed down the toilet.

Look at the route you take to work each day. Are you heading towards your fame (south), prosperity (southeast), or career (north) direction? If not, see if you can change your route so that at least part of it has you heading in the right direction.

If you own your own business, you have some control over your work environment. Most people work for others and have no say in the choice or location of the building they work in. Naturally, the best building for you is one that faces either your element or your career direction.

Usually, you will have some control over your immediate working environment. Evaluate your office carefully. Is it in an auspicious part of the building? (The very best location is at the farthest diagonal corner from the entrance. This is usually where the owner or manager has his or her office.) Is it regular in shape? Does the door open to a good direction for you? Ideally, your office door will be in the career sector. If it is not, are you able to make changes?

Is your desk in a good location? For career advancement, the best position is in the career or fame sectors. Once your desk is sited in a good area, place it so that you are facing another auspicious direction. This means that you will think well and make good decisions while seated at your desk. As there are so many things to be aware of, it is not always easy to find a good position.

Naturally, you should avoid sitting with your back towards the window as you lack the support of a solid wall behind you. You must not sit with your back to the door, either, as you do not want to be "stabbed in the back." You also do not want your desk or chair to be directly under any exposed beams. A friend of mine used to suffer from constant headaches caused by a beam over his desk. Once he changed the layout of his office the headaches completely disappeared. If the most auspicious direction can not be used because of these problems, try the second best position.

To enhance your progress, place a metal object in the career sector of your office. This could be a metal wind chime, an ornament of gold or silver, an aquarium made of glass and metal, or simply a few coins.

A friend of mine was given a large brass elephant, which his wife hated. He took it to work and placed it in the career sector of his office and was promoted within four months.

He has had several more promotions since, and now his wife complains that he pays more attention to the elephant than he does to her.

The desk should be of sufficient size to reflect your status and position. In feng shui there are lucky and unlucky dimensions based on a unit of seventeen inches. This is divided into eight sections, four of which are lucky and four unlucky. The first, fourth, fifth, and eighth sections are considered lucky.[1] Naturally, the height, width, and length of your desk should all be lucky measurements.

The lucky measurements are: between zero and $2\frac{1}{8}$ inches, between 6 and $10\frac{5}{8}$ inches, between 17 and $19\frac{1}{8}$ inches, between $23\frac{3}{8}$ and $27\frac{5}{8}$ inches, between $31\frac{3}{4}$ and $36\frac{1}{8}$ inches, between $40\frac{3}{8}$ and $44\frac{5}{8}$ inches, between $48\frac{3}{4}$ and $53\frac{1}{8}$ inches, between $57\frac{3}{8}$ and $61\frac{5}{8}$ inches, and between $65\frac{3}{4}$ and 68 inches.

Consequently, good measurements for a desk would be: 33 inches high, 60 inches long, and 36 inches wide. In Hong Kong a great deal of furniture is made according to lucky measurements.[2]

Check the other items of furniture in your office. Ensure that they also conform to lucky measurements. Be careful that the individual shelves of bookcases do not become poison arrows. Remove or change the position of anything that has a sharp edge or corner pointing at you.

The feng shui of your home is more important than that of your work place. However, if you improve both you will make your path that much smoother and easier.

Prosperity Aids for Business

Chinese business people are an intriguing mix of shrewdness, intelligence, and superstition. There are many things that they do to increase the potential for success, and, generally speaking, they are highly successful in business.

Naturally, they use feng shui to give them an extra edge over their competitors, and some of this has been mentioned in the previous chapter. They also use other devices that appear to help as well. These might be called superstitions in the West, but it is interesting to note that we are now starting to use some of the ideas that have been used in the East for thousands of years. Affirmations are a good example.

In the East it is not uncommon to see eight coins tied together in a chain with red thread hanging on a wall. These act as talismans and are believed to attract good luck and prosperity. Seeing the display of coins regularly also acts as a visual prompt to the businessperson as to why he or she is in business. Many businesspeople carry an old coin around with them to attract luck. Some even have coins sewn into their garments so that they have an old coin on them at all times. The most popular coins date from the Tang and Sung dynasties (618–905 C.E. and 960–1279 C.E.). Replicas of these coins can frequently be found at import stores.

Beautiful examples of calligraphy often adorn the walls of Chinese business premises. They usually contain affirmations designed to keep the staff motivated and to attract money to the business.

Pictures and statues of the Chinese gods of wealth are often strategically located in the business premises, again to attract money into the business. There are several gods of wealth, but the one most frequently seen is Tsai Shen Yeh. Laughing Buddhas are sometimes seen as well, and the owners of the business will reverently stroke his stomach every day to attract good luck.

None of these things constitute feng shui, even though they are sometimes associated with it. However, they do enable the business owner to remain motivated and to keep his or her eyes firmly on the goal of not only a profit, but also wealth and abundance.

8

Feng Shui in the Home

We can't all live in the perfect position surrounded by the green dragon and white tiger. Most of us live in cities and frequently other buildings have to serve as our dragons and tigers. However, we can do a great deal inside our homes to make them as beneficial as possible from a feng shui point of view.

The Front Door

If possible, your front door should be in the left-hand side of the front of your house. It can be in the middle, but try and avoid having it on the right-hand side. This is because the left side belongs to the green dragon, and ideally we want his energy and beneficial ch'i to surround and enter the house through the front door.

The door should also be in proportion to the rest of the house. Friends of ours have a small house with a gigantic front door that would be more in keeping with a small castle than a cottage. Extremely large or tall front doors create financial problems, which our friends have suffered. Extremely small front doors tend to stifle the occupants, creating arguments and disharmony. The front door should always be larger than the back door.

We have already discussed the external shars dealing with the front door. You have to deal with poison arrows at your front door. This is the most important single factor in feng shui. These start with the driveway itself. As negative ch'i flows in straight lines, avoid a drive that heads in a straight line directly to your front door. Also, the drive should not be narrower than the front door, or wider at the house end than at the road. This situation stifles financial opportunities. Driveways should also not slope steeply downward and away from the house, as this siphons off money and ch'i.

Check your environment for shars attacking your front door. These could be created by the roof lines of nearby houses, fences, retaining walls, telephone or power poles, a steep hill, large buildings, or other large structures.

These shars can be eliminated by planting trees to block out the offending poison arrow. You need to plant a few trees, as a single tree can ultimately become a shar itself. The trees ideally need to be evergreen and have broad leaves, rather than pointed ones. Naturally, trees take time to grow, so a short-term remedy would be to use a pa-kua mirror over the door to deflect the poison arrows.

A large wall can conceal some shars, such as a road heading directly towards your front door. Another remedy is to change the direction of your front door, so that it is no longer pointing directly at the shar.

The front door should open into a wide, well-lit entrance foyer. It should reveal, rather than conceal, part of the interior of the house. The entrance should be welcoming and give a feeling of happiness and well-being. A small, cramped, gloomy entrance prevents ch'i from entering, and causes illness and money problems. An entrance like this can be helped with bright lights and a large mirror. If the entrance foyer is too large, a screen can be used to make it appear smaller.

If the front door opens directly onto a wall, or a narrow entrance, use a mirror and lights to make the entrance more appealing.

The front door should not directly face either the front door of the house across the road or your own front gate.

The front door should not face a staircase, as it is believed that ch'i goes straight up the stairs and dissipates.

The front door should not face the back door. This sometimes happens in houses with a long hallway going right through the middle of the house. When this happens, ch'i enters the front door and goes straight out through the back. The front door should not face the door of a toilet or bedroom. In fact, the toilet, stove, and fireplace should not be visible from the front door.

If the front door is made of two panels, they should be the same size.

Do not leave the front door open when the wind is blowing towards it, as the wind will "blow" money and good luck out of the house.

The room that the front door faces has a bearing on the entire family, even if the room cannot be seen because of an intervening wall. If the front door faces the dining room, family life will be happy and convivial. If the front door faces the family room, the occupants will be close to each other and enjoy spending time in each other's company. If the front door faces a room containing a television set, the people living there will waste a great deal of time.

If the front door faces the kitchen, the occupants will tend to eat too much. If the front door faces a bedroom, the occupants will always be tired and lacking in energy. If the front door faces a study, the occupants will be industrious. If the front door faces a toilet, the occupants will remain poor as the wealth will be flushed away.

The Staircase

The staircase is important as it connects the upstairs and downstairs ch'i and, hopefully, aids the flow of ch'i to every corner of the house.

Staircases should flow in a gentle curve, rather than in a straight line. Spiral stairs are hard for ch'i to negotiate, and should be avoided. The banisters should not contain any sharp corners, either.

The number of steps in the staircase is considered important. They are counted in groups of three or four. The three-step cycle is: gold, silver, and death. The four-step cycle is: good luck, prosperity, bad luck, and failure. Naturally, the last step should be gold, silver, good luck, or prosperity. Consequently, the ideal number of steps are: one, two, five, ten, thirteen, fourteen, seventeen, twenty-two, twenty-five, twenty-six, and twenty-nine.

The staircase should not face the front door, the toilet door, or a bedroom door, nor should it be placed in the exact center of the house. The center is known as the Good Luck position, and the good luck is entirely wasted if this position is used for the staircase.

The staircase should not be too steep, too narrow, or spiral. It should gently curve. A landing halfway up the staircase is regarded as being good.

The staircase should be well lit to encourage ch'i to flow upstairs and downstairs.

Each step of the staircase should be solid and attached to the next step. Stairs with an open space between each step confuse the ch'i and make it hard to move in either direction.

The Living Room

The living room should be a comfortable, pleasant room where people feel relaxed and happy. It is the room where the family congregates, and where guests are entertained.

The living room should be in proportion to the other rooms of the house. It should be regular in shape. It should receive some sunlight through the windows. However, there should not be a window directly facing the main entrance to the room. The living room should not be over-filled with furniture and ornaments, which give it a crowded look.

The living room should not be on a lower level to the rest of the house.

Square and oblong-shaped living rooms are considered ideal. Long, narrow living rooms should be well lit. Mirrors should be placed on one of the long sides to make the room look better balanced. If the room is wide and narrow, with the main entrance on the wide side, chairs should be placed beside this door.

The living room should not contain any exposed beams. Exposed beams are very bad feng shui, creating the feeling of having a large weight on one's shoulders. Exposed beams constrict ch'i, which in turn constricts the family's finances and happiness. A remedy is to lower the ceiling so that the exposed beams are concealed. A cheaper remedy is to attach a small pa-kua to the center of the beam. Alternatively, two small flutes with tassels can be hung from the beam.

The living room should reflect the personality of the people who live in the house. Consequently, examples of their interests, such as books, models, certificates, photographs, and so on, should be in view. A feature can be made of collections of objects. My mother used to collect antique ceramic chickens sitting on baskets. She had these displayed on a bookcase in her living room. The sun caught these for part of the day, reflecting the cheerful colors and brightening the entire room. This helped to create beneficial ch'i.

The furniture should be in keeping with the personality of the occupants and the size and shape of the room. It should be comfortable. The chair that the head of the family sits in should face the main entrance to the living room.

Some of the furniture needs to be round in shape to eliminate sharp corners. Round side tables, round rugs, round lamps and chandeliers, and any other items with rounded corners are considered beneficial. The Chinese consider round shapes to be a symbol of money.

Chinese families usually have affirmations in the form of calligraphy of the wall, and ornaments representing prosperity, good health, and long life in their living rooms.

The Bedroom

The feng shui of the bedroom is extremely important. We spend at least a third of our lives in bed; consequently, we spend more time in our bedroom than anywhere else in the house. The master bedroom should be as far away from the front door as possible, ideally diagonal across the house from it. This symbolically gives the occupants more security and allows them to sleep better.

The placement of the bed is of vital importance. (Apart from the front door, the placement of the bed and the stove are the most important factors in residential feng shui.) The bed should be placed in such a position that a person lying in bed can see anyone coming in through the door. Ideally, the bed should be placed as near as possible to the corner diagonally opposite the door. The foot of the bed should not point directly at the door, as this reminds the Chinese of coffins lined up in a mortuary. It is known as the "death" position.

The bed should not lie directly underneath an exposed beam. If the occupant is lying under an exposed beam he or she is likely to become ill in the part of the body that is directly below the beam. For instance, if the beam went over the stomach area, the person would be likely to experience stomach cramps. If it passed over the occupant's head, he or she could experience headaches. If there is no alternative place for the bed, ensure that the beam runs the length of the bed, rather than across it.

The headboard of the bed should be in contact with a wall. One side of the bed can also be in contact with the adjacent wall if desired. If the bed is not touching a wall, the occupant will feel unsettled and unstable.

The bed should not face a mirror, though mirrors in other positions are beneficial. Mirrors facing the bed put great strains on a marriage. However, mirrors can be extremely important if, for some reason, the placement of the bed does not allow the person lying in bed to see who is entering the room. A mirror placed in the correct position to allow the entrance to be seen removes this difficulty.

The bed should be in a position that gives the occupant a pleasant view when waking. A window providing a pleasant outlook would be ideal. However, the bed should not receive direct sunlight. Be careful that there are no outside shars that could come in through the window. If any of these are present, they can be blocked off by using heavy drapes.

Large chests of drawers or bureaus should not be placed next to the bed as they are believed to upset the flow of ch'i.

Whenever possible, the bed should be in the direction indicated by the pa-kua. This direction is determined by whatever it is you want. However, the Health and Longevity directions are usually considered most favorable here (see Chapter 3).

The bed should not be moved while the wife is pregnant, nor should the area under the bed be dusted or cleaned during this period. This is because the Chinese believe that

Ling, molecular-sized spirits, are waiting under the bed to enter the unborn baby and provide it with the breath of life (ch'i). The rooms of newly born babies should be checked for adverse shars, as they make the babies unhappy and cause them to cry constantly.

The color of the carpet and wallpaper in the bedrooms should be compatible with the occupant's element. This is particularly important in children's bedrooms.

- If the child's element is wood/green, a suitable room color is blue.
- If the child's element is fire/red, a suitable room color is green.
- If the child's element is earth/yellow or brown, a suitable room color is red.
- If the child's element is metal/white, a suitable room color is yellow.
- If the child's element is water/blue or black, a suitable room color is white.

The Kitchen

Many feng shui practitioners consider the kitchen to be the most important room in the house, as it contains the stove and symbolizes the wealth of the family.

The kitchen should be well lit, spacious, and airy. Fresh air and good light are essential for promoting ch'i, which will then enter the freshly cooked meal, benefitting the whole family. The quantity and quality of the food is related to the family's prosperity. Consequently, it is a matter of pride to always have food in the larder and refrigerator.

The stove (or oven or microwave) is the most important item in the kitchen. It should be placed so that the person using it will not have his or her back towards the kitchen entrance. If the cook is surprised by people entering the kitchen, his or her nerves will be affected, thus affecting the quality of the food. A mirror can be used, if necessary, to enable the cook to see anyone entering the kitchen.

A Chinese restaurant at which my wife and I frequently eat has mirrors entirely surrounding the stove. The cook says that he hates not knowing what people are doing behind his back, and installed the mirrors so that he knows exactly what is going on in every part of the kitchen. However, though he would not admit this to us, mirrors around and behind the stove create a more peaceful environment. Also, they have the effect of symbolically multiplying the number of stove elements, which gives him the potential to make much more money.

There should be enough room around the stove to enable the cook to work comfortably without feeling cramped. The stove should be kept clean and work properly. Frustrations caused by a stove that does not work the way it should create negative ch'i. Symbolically, the kitchen, and particularly the stove, represents family wealth. It should be clean and work well to stimulate the family's finances.

It is natural that the kitchen symbolizes wealth. If the occupants are well fed with good quality food, they will be able to function effectively in the real world and make money. If the quality and quantity of the food is poor, they will not have the energy to earn much money.

The stove should not face the front door, the toilet door, or the door of the master bedroom. It should not be placed under a beam or in a corner, nor should it face a staircase or a bed. The kitchen door should not face either the front or back doors.

Any drains in the kitchen (and toilet) should be concealed. This is because in feng shui it is not considered good to watch the water leave.

If the house is two or more stories high, a toilet should not be placed directly above the kitchen as this will adversely affect the occupants' wealth and good luck.

The level of the kitchen floor should be the same as that of the dining room.

The Dining Room

The dining room should be of sufficient size to comfortably accommodate the dining table. It should be near the kitchen, but not close to the front door. If it is too close, your guests will eat their meals quickly and then leave. A screen to hide the front door acts as a feng shui remedy in this situation. The dining room should be placed in a corner of the house, if possible, allowing windows on two sides to increase the amount of ch'i.

Frequently, the dining room is an alcove or corner of the living room. This is fine, as it is important for the dining area to receive plenty of ch'i energy. However, the dining table should not point towards the front door, even if it is situated diagonally across the room from the front door.

The dining table should be square, oblong, oval, round, or pa-kua shaped. It is even better if the square and oblong tables have rounded corners. Round tables are favored as this allows everyone sitting at the table to converse easily with everyone else. This enhances the ch'i energies of the room.

The most favored tables are made from wood or wood and metal. Glass or marble-topped tables should be avoided.

The dining table should not be placed under an exposed beam, nor should it face a staircase or toilet door.

Additional furniture, such as side tables, dresser, and sideboard are welcome as long as they do not make the room feel cramped. It is important for the room to feel spacious, to enhance the feelings of abundance and well-being.

Mirrors serve to symbolically double the amount of food being offered and are very welcome in this room. They can also serve to make a small dining room appear larger.

Chinese families like to have intricately carved furniture in this room. A common motif is the dragon and pearl. Frequently, figures of the three Taoist gods of prosperity, happiness, and longevity are displayed in this room.

The Study

You are considered fortunate if you have a room to act as a study in your home. This is because the study provides a quiet place to sit and work or to simply relax. Your study should reflect you and your personality. The furniture should be comfortable and the room should contain sufficient lighting.

Pictures on the wall, especially ones showing mountains, lakes, and rivers, are believed to increase creativity and provide inspiration.

The Toilet

Toilets should be as inconspicuous as possible. They should not be placed in significant areas of the house, such as the wealth, fame, or career sectors. Symbolically, a toilet in these positions "flushes" away every opportunity.

The toilet should be situated on the side of the house, rather than in a central position. The negative ch'i from a centrally located toilet spreads throughout the house.

Toilets should not be too large. It is preferable to have the toilet as a separate room to the bathroom. If they are combined, separate the two with a half wall. This means it will not be seen by other users of the bathroom and the negative ch'i energy is dissipated. Also, it provides the users with a degree of privacy.

The Bathroom

Both the toilet and bathroom are places where water (money) is used. As a result these rooms symbolize the occupants' financial position. Consequently, it is important that they be positioned with great care.

The bathroom should not be visible from the front door, or be in the wealth location. It should be well ventilated, well lit, and kept thoroughly clean. It should be decorated with delicate colors to maintain domestic harmony.

Mirrors are beneficial, and usually necessary, in the bathroom. Avoid mirrored walls made from numerous square tiles. These form a netting type effect that constricts the money flow.

9

Designing Your Own Home

You are very fortunate if you have the opportunity to design and build your own home, as you can incorporate feng shui principles at every stage.

If possible, choose a square or rectangular-shaped section on a plot that slopes slightly towards the road. It is even better if you can find a site that faces clean water. Harbour, sea, lake, or river views are all good, and symbolize prosperity.

Seek out the green dragon and the white tiger and position your house so that the front door faces your most important direction. Many feng shui masters ignore this, saying that all houses should face south in the northern hemisphere. This is because for thousands of years they have noticed that success, wealth, and happiness come to people who live facing the sun. Naturally, if you follow these precepts, your house should face north if you live in the southern hemisphere. This allows the maximum amount of sunlight to enter and warm the house. (I live in the southern hemisphere, and the number of houses that have been built in the last five years using feng shui principles, yet aligned to the northern hemisphere, rather than the southern, has been amazing. This happened because many of the houses were designed by architects living in the northern hemisphere. This no longer occurs in my city, but it meant a large number of houses were sold again only months after the new residents had moved in.)

Although you want sunlight, you also want a balance of yin and yang energy. You do not want a site that is exposed all day long to the heat of the sun, but neither do you want a site that is shaded much of the time by nearby hills or tall buildings. The area should not be totally flat, but neither should it be too steep. It should be neither too dry nor too damp. We look for balance in feng shui.

Evaluate your potential site carefully to see if any poison arrows affect it. It is particularly important that no poison arrows affect your front door. Look at neighbouring buildings and roads. Is your site situated at a junction of two or more roads? Do any roads point directly at your site? Are there overhead power lines? Is the site near a church, police station, prison, or hospital? Is there a large hill or large building directly in front of your piece of land?

Are there any rivers or waterways situated nearby? These should be in front of your section, rather than behind it. They also should contain clean water, rather than dirty or polluted water. Is the water moving or is it stagnant?

Does the vegetation in the area look vigorous and healthy? This indicates an abundance of good ch'i. Naturally, you will want your soil to be fertile, receive plenty of sunlight, and have good drainage.

Ask questions about your site. You should avoid places where a murder or violence of another type has occurred. The feng shui is also bad if the previous house burned down. The site should also be avoided if it is on reclaimed land that was built on top of garbage.

Once you have found the right section, design a house that is regular in shape and build it in the center of your site. This means that both the front and back gardens will be similar in size.

Your property should contain a circular or curving driveway leading to the house. If you have to have a straight driveway, ensure that it does not head directly to your front door.

Design your house using the date of birth of the head of the house. The layout should "flow" to allow the ch'i to enter the front door and effortlessly pass through to every part of the house. There should be no obstacles or obstructions to hinder the free flow of ch'i energy. This creates a happy, healthy environment for everyone living in the house.

The house should be well balanced, both inside and out. It should harmonize with the outside environment. It should not be too large or small for the size of the land. It should not cast shars on to neighbouring properties. An extremely large house, for instance, will have a negative effect on nearby houses. Sharply angled roofs have the potential to be very bad shars. Be aware that if you do send poison arrows to other houses they can use remedies and send these shars straight back to you.

Choose attractive materials to build with, and choose these using your personal elements. In Taiwan it is customary to place "five lucky objects" under the foundation posts when building. These are usually five small coins, but can be anything that could be considered lucky. A small pa-kua would suffice. It is claimed that these increase the quality of the ch'i and bring luck and good fortune to all the occupants of the house.

Balance applies inside the house as well. The rooms should be airy and not too small. The room shapes should be regular and the rooms should be neither disproportionately large nor small for their function. It is bad feng shui to design a house with an enormous living room and tiny bedrooms. Each room should be in balance with the others.

Avoid L-shaped rooms as these symbolize a butcher's cleaver and create problems for the occupants. Avoid sloping ceilings for the same reason.

The front door should open into an attractive lobby that is reasonably private, but still gives a good view of the interior of the house. If the entrance is too narrow the amount of ch'i able to enter your home is restricted. The rooms nearest the front door should be the living room and study. This projects a feeling of relaxation and harmony to visitors when they first enter.

The kitchen should not be placed by the front door. This creates excessive emphasis on food and the occupants would gain weight. If your guests see a bedroom as soon as they enter your home, they will immediately feel tired and want to rest. Naturally, the very worst room for your guests to see as they enter is the toilet and bathroom. This affects the occupants' health.

Avoid split-level homes, if possible. If your home is split-level make sure that the living room is not higher than the dining room and kitchen. When it is, all the beneficial ch'i will flow into your visitors and depart with them. It is also very bad ch'i to locate the bedrooms, recreation rooms, and study on a higher level than the dining room.

Avoid having three or more doors in a row. This allows the ch'i to flow through too quickly and the beneficial effects are lost. In effect, three or more doors create an internal shar that can lead to emotional problems and difficulties within the family.

Doors in a hallway should not directly face another door. This is even more important if one door is larger than the other, as the large door overpowers the smaller one. Avoid slanting doors. This is a door where the top is not square to the sides, but is cut on a bias or angle. It is normally found in houses with sloping ceilings. This type of door symbolizes an axe and creates very bad feng shui.

You should have plenty of windows in your house to encourage ch'i. However, you should not have more than three times as many windows as doors. The windows should open outward, as this allows the maximum amount of ch'i to come in. Windows that slide up, and windows that open halfway, restrict the amount of ch'i entering the house. This has a limiting effect on the careers and finances of the family.

Exposed beams are quite fashionable in some types of homes. As you already know, exposed beams are considered extremely bad shars and should be avoided in your home. Diamond-paned windows are often found in homes with exposed beams. They have the effect of restricting the amount of ch'i that can enter the home and they can make a bad shar even worse.

Avoid projecting corners as these create shars. Be particularly aware that these can sometimes occur with certain types of ceilings, and are not restricted solely to walls. Try also to avoid square-shaped columns, as each corner will send out poison arrows. Round columns are much less harmful.

If your house contains stairs, ensure that the staircase is broad and curves gently. It should not face the front door, and the stairs should not be made up of individual, separated steps, but be a complete unit of interconnected steps.

Use the pa-kua or Lo Shu magic square to lay out your house. By doing this, you can allocate particular parts of the house to different members of the family, and also align the rooms correctly.

The dining room should be large enough to comfortably accommodate the table and other furniture. A large mirror can apparently double the amount of food being served. A spacious feeling in this room gives feelings of expansion and good luck.

The kitchen should be next to the dining room. It should be well lit and spacious. The stove needs to be well sited, also. Put a great deal of thought into the placement and design of your kitchen as this room is the source of your wealth in feng shui. In the traditional Form School of feng shui, south and east have always been considered good directions for the kitchen, but southwest should be avoided.

The bedrooms should not be aligned in a row along a passageway. Long hallways are considered bad in feng shui, and all the doors from the bedrooms will create disharmony and strife.

The toilet and bathroom should be private and not visible from the front door. It also should not be sited at the end of a long hallway or directly opposite another door. Like the kitchen, think carefully about the placement of the toilet. It should be placed along an outside wall, rather than in the center of the house. This allows it to have a window, which enables light and ch'i to enter. A windowless toilet is called a "dead" toilet, and it is essential for a room like this to contain a large mirror to stimulate and encourage ch'i energy.

Symbolically, the toilet is where good fortune and wealth get flushed away. Consequently, the toilet should not be placed in the north or southeast sectors of the house, as these are the career and wealth areas. In feng shui it is considered good etiquette, and simple common sense, to keep the toilet and bathroom doors closed.

There are many methods of deciding where each room should go. We have already looked at the pa-kua method and the Lo Shu magic square.

In Hong Kong houses are frequently designed using the eight corners of the pa-kua as directions. Naturally, whenever possible, the house will face south and sit north. The study or office, for instance, should be placed in the southeast (wealth sector). The workrooms, office, or study should be in the south (fame sector). The daughters of the family should use the rooms in the southwest (marriage sector). Young children should make use of the rooms in the west (children sector). Older children should use the northwest part of the house (mentors sector). Teenage children should use rooms in the north (career sector). The children's places of study should be in the northeast (knowledge sector). The master bedroom should be placed in the east (family sector). Refer to Chapter 3 for how the trigrams of the pa-kua indicate the different members of the family.

In traditional feng shui, the house always faced south and all of the most important rooms faced this direction as well. The front door always faced south, too. The kitchen faced east, and the rooms of the older members of the family faced southeast.

The outside landscaping needs to be done with care to harmonize and balance the house. A swimming pool can be an excellent source of ch'i and wealth, as water represents money. The pool should contain curves, rather than sharp angles. The pool should not be so large that it appears to overpower the house. Surround the pool with attractive landscaping to help it blend into the environment. A fish pond also encourages beneficial ch'i. In addition to the water, any goldfish will symbolize money.

Decorative rock gardens symbolize mountains and protect the occupants of the house. Choose the larger boulders with care and ensure that they do not send any shars towards the house.

Because trees symbolize strength and honesty, trees and shrubs, particularly evergreens, increase the amount of ch'i, and can also serve as the green dragon and white tiger if your house is on level ground. If you use them for this purpose, ensure that the trees on the right-hand side as you leave your front door are slightly higher than the trees on the other side. Trees planted behind your house serve to protect it. Avoid large numbers of trees in front of your house, especially directly in front of your main door.

Maintain balance in your garden. An extremely large tree that dwarfs everything else in your garden upsets the balance and harmony.

Flower gardens can increase the levels of ch'i. Colorful flowers symbolize progress, happiness, and longevity.

If you choose your site carefully and build the house of your dreams on it using feng shui principles, you and your family will lead a life of happiness and prosperity.

10

Feng Shui in the Garden

Chinese gardens have been designed and laid out by feng shui principles for at least 3,000 years.[1] Early Western visitors to China were impressed with the quality of these gardens and the elegant pagodas they often contained. In fact, it was frequently the pagodas that aroused their initial curiosity about feng shui. This is because the pagodas were originally erected to increase the feng shui of the surrounding countryside.[2] Small porcelain pagodas are still frequently found as ornamentation in Chinese gardens.

We have already discussed some of the things that can be done in the garden to improve our feng shui. We can plant trees, add a stream or fountain, or add boulders, walls, and paths to enhance our ch'i and make our environments more pleasant and beneficial. However, we can do much more than this. Start by placing a pa-kua over a plan of your garden. Each direction relates to you.

- The southern part of your plot is related to your fame, standing in the community, and personal power. The colors are red and orange.

- The southeast is concerned with money and wealth. The colors are red, green, blue, and purple.
- The east relates to health. The colors are brown and green.
- The northeast is related to knowledge and learning. The colors are green, blue, and black.
- The north is concerned with your career. The colors are clear (as in water), blue, and black.
- The northwest area is related to benefactors and travel. The colors are white, gray, and black.
- The west is concerned with children, pets, and creativity. The colors are white and silver.
- The southwest is related to love and marriage. The colors are red, pink, and white.

Flowers

We can plant flowers of any color anywhere, but if we wish to activate a certain area of our lives we should plant flowers of the correct color in the correct location of our garden. The size of the garden is not important. It may just be a window box. Simply plant the correct flowers in the right place and look after them.

Many people dislike dandelions in their lawns. However, dandelions are considered highly beneficial in feng shui. They are believed to protect family members from accidents and keep them in good health. They also symbolize money. (For some inexplicable reason my wife will not allow me to use the feng shui benefits of dandelions as an excuse not to mow our lawns!)

Geraniums are also a highly beneficial feng shui flower. Red ones are believed to attract prosperity. Naturally, these should be planted in the southeast part of your garden, but may also be planted on each side of your front and back doors. White geraniums are believed to grant peace of mind and encourage pleasant dreams.

Holly attracts money, making it a good plant to place in the southeast.

Jasmine symbolizes friendship and affection. It should be planted in the northwest or east.

Hollyhock is a symbol of fertility and should be planted in the west and southwest by couples wanting children. Pomegranates also symbolize fertility.

Daffodils should be planted in the northeast to encourage open-mindedness, generosity, and communication. Plant them sparingly though, as too many are believed to dissipate your energies.

Cornflowers enable you to establish and maintain balance in your relationships. They can be planted anywhere you feel you need these energies. The most usual position is in the northwest and southwest.

Roses are usually beneficial. White roses enable you to see the essentials of a situation. Yellow ones encourage intellectual discussions and learning. Red roses symbolize beauty, but can also, if overdone in a garden, be related to vanity and bickering. They should be planted in the south section of your garden. An odd number of rose bushes is preferred.

Tulips, especially red ones, symbolize love. They should be planted in the southwest and east.

Begonias symbolize partnerships and healthy children. They should be planted in the west.

Flowers of any color are regarded as being beneficial and encourage an abundance of ch'i energy. The best ones to choose are those that contain plenty of flowers and lush foliage. Long-lived plants are preferred as they symbolize prosperity, longevity, and good health.

Don't forget to include in your garden some of the five favorite flowers of feng shui: peonies, chrysanthemums, magnolias, orchids, and lotus. Refer to Chapter 6 for the meanings of these flowers.

Fruit Trees

Fruit trees all symbolize different things in feng shui. Apples, apricots, pomegranates, and persimmons symbolize fertility and fruitfulness. Peach trees symbolize friendship, love, and immortality. Pear trees symbolize longevity and prosperity. Plums symbolize youthfulness and vitality. Oranges symbolize good fortune, wealth, and happiness.

Other Considerations

Other aspects of your garden need to be considered, also. The main paths in your garden should be in the western side. They should not be in straight lines, but meander. This symbolizes a long life.

Trees should be planted in the east and southeast for strength and protection. Naturally, they can be planted anywhere to act as a screen or to block off a shar.

Streams are highly beneficial and symbolize wealth. If you are fortunate enough to have one, look after it and ensure that the water stays fresh, creating an abundance of ch'i.

Ponds symbolize success. They should be placed in the south or east, and stocked with an odd number of goldfish. A rockery around part of the pond is highly beneficial, particularly if it contains a small waterfall.

Finally, your garden must be pleasing to you when you look at it. Plant the correct plants for the things that you wish to improve in your life, but also include plants that you simply enjoy. Hide from view any shars coming from outside your property to make your garden a safe, secure haven where you can relax, unwind, and enjoy being in harmony with the earth.

11

Feng Shui in the Work Place

Most of us spend at least forty hours a week at work. We are much more productive and contented when our work environment is pleasant and happy. Naturally, our work environment should be as harmonious as possible. The design should allow ch'i to flow freely throughout the building. Good feng shui encourages harmonious relationships between the people working in the premises. Fortunately, we can do a great deal to create this environment using feng shui.

First of all, we need an office that is sited in the right position for us. When the door of our office is in the K'an (career) section, the main entrance to the building should be facing the wealth and fame areas of our pa-kua.

The office building should not be at the end of a no-exit road, or have any other type of shar attacking it. Look carefully for any straight lines or sharp angles that could be attacking you. Office buildings are often surrounded by other large office blocks and these should be examined to ensure that they are not aiming poison arrows in your

Figure 11: A small office building between two larger buildings is not a good location.

direction. It is also not good to be housed in a small office building between two much larger buildings (Figure 11).

If the building is standing in your own grounds you can plant trees to protect yourself and increase the amount of ch'i. Trees planted behind the building serve as protection. Trees on the right and left sides can act as the green dragon and white tiger. The trees on the right-hand side as you leave the front door should be slightly higher and larger than the ones on the other side. You can also include a fountain to create a wealth of beneficial ch'i for your business. If a river flows past your premises it should be in front of your building and not behind it. A river behind your building indicates financial opportunities that float away and cannot be utilized.

If you are constructing your own building, you can design one that harmonizes with the environment and the buildings that are already there. You can position your building to attract good ch'i and to eliminate as many potential shars as possible. Try to construct your building so that when you are looking out the land on the right side of your front door is higher than that on the left. Naturally, this helps create a symbolic dragon and tiger. Ideally, you should also orientate the building so that it is facing gently flowing water. Finally, it would be wonderful if the back of your building was protected by a hill or taller building.

The entrance to your building is very important. It should be in keeping with the building as a whole, and ideally should face the wealth direction. It should appear welcoming, but not be too large in comparison with the rest of the building. It should be well lit to encourage ch'i energy. If the lobby or foyer is small, a large mirror can help create a feeling of spaciousness. If your receptionist is stationed in the lobby, he or she should not be placed at a desk that directly faces the front door.

Revolving doors create beneficial ch'i and do not cast shars on neighbouring buildings.

Try to avoid offices that directly face escalators and elevators, because they can carry all the wealth away. Do not site your office at the end of a long hallway. The hallway itself will act as a poison arrow, harming your work, wealth, and ultimately your career. Do not choose an office that opens directly onto a toilet on the other side of the hallway.

The offices themselves should be square or oblong in shape. Unusual shapes should be avoided, particularly L-shaped offices, as these look like a meat cleaver. We do not want pillars or large beams in the office, nor do we want protruding corners or sharp edges created by room dividers and desks. Some sharp angles are unavoidable, but can usually be concealed by mirrors and potted plants.

Office doors that face other office doors should align perfectly to avoid tension and disagreements.

All electrical and telephone cables should be out of sight.

The office of the manager, owner, or director should be positioned carefully, as the success of the enterprise depends on his or her good feng shui. Traditionally, the southeast is considered to be the wealth and prosperity sector. Alternatively, that office should be as far away as possible from the entrance. A corner position, diagonally opposite to the entrance, will enable the boss to receive respect and to maintain control of the business.

The boss' office should be larger than the other offices to signify this person's superior status. It should be well lit, and be square or oblong in shape. The room should contain decorations that enhance the element of its occupant. For instance, if he or she has wood as the main element, the office should contain a plant. If the element is water, a small aquarium would be beneficial. A bright light would benefit a fire person, as would a painting that included plenty of red in it. A metal wind chime would help someone whose element is metal. Finally, a quartz crystal would enhance the potential of an earth person.

The size of the boss' desk is also important. It should reflect his or her status and be large, but not too large in proportion to the size of the office. A desk five feet long and three feet wide is a good size for the managing director or president. Naturally, the other desks in the company should be smaller, the actual size being determined by the seniority of the person using it. The desks of secretaries should not be L-shaped, but be oblong or curving. The receptionist's desk should always be a curving one.

The position of your desk in the office is vitally important. You should not sit with your back to the door. This makes it too easy for others to "stab you in the back." You also should not have your back towards the window, as this indicates a lack of support. You will be betrayed or let down by your colleagues.

Ideally, you should sit facing the door. You can choose the best placement by aligning a pa-kua over a plan of your office and choosing the most auspicious direction.

General offices housing several people should be well lit and designed to encourage the flow of ch'i energy. The desks should be sited carefully to ensure that they do not send shars to the other people in the room. Plants can help to hide potential shars and at the same time create beneficial ch'i.

It is important to design general offices with care as the final result will have a lot to do with the level of absenteeism and productivity of the occupants.

The color scheme of the office is important, too. Subtle colors are better than extremely bright, stimulating ones. Extremely bright colors will cause discord with some of the visitors to your office. Use the element relating to your year of birth to determine the best color for you.

You can also use the productive cycle of the five elements (Figure 1D, page 16) to choose suitable colors for your office. For instance, following the productive cycle, we see that:

- Fire is good for earth. If your element is earth, you might include some red in your color scheme.

- Earth is good for metal. If your element is metal, you could benefit by incorporating some brown or beige into your color scheme.

- Metal is good for water. If your element is water, you might choose to use some white or gold in your color scheme.

- Water is good for wood. If your element is wood, you could incorporate blue or black into your color scheme.

- Wood is good for fire. If your element is fire, you might use different shades of green in your color scheme.

Shops and stores should follow the same principles. If you are contemplating leasing a store in a mall, make sure that you do not select one at the end of a corridor. This may appear to be an excellent location as all the potential customers will head directly towards you, but in reality, the corridor will act as a poison arrow. Consequently, even though a particular building may seem to have excellent feng shui, there will always be places inside the building to avoid.

If you own a shop in a row of similar stores, ensure that your store front is similar in size to the others. If your store front is noticeably narrower, your business will be adversely affected by the neighbouring stores. If your store front is wider than your neighbours' store fronts, you will gain increased trade at their expense.

A friend of mine owned a store that sold both woolen garments and souvenirs. He did reasonably well for many years, until he decided to turn his store into two separate stores, one selling the garments and the other the souvenirs. He thought this would help his business, but in fact, the opposite occurred. Instead of one large frontage, he ended up with two small frontages, and his volume of business declined markedly. Business improved only after he returned his store to what it had originally been.

The sales staff should face the door and welcome potential customers with a pleasant smile. Your merchandise should be attractively displayed to encourage sales. The display cabinets or counters inside the store should not point towards the door as this creates a shar that stops potential customers from coming in.

A mirror beside your cash register symbolically doubles all of the money as it goes into the register. The cash register should not face the entrance directly, but be at an angle to it. In Hong Kong, Malaysia, and Taiwan a metal or wooden wind chime is often hung over the cash register. This encourages the ch'i to rise and bring more business into the store. It is vitally important that no poison arrows are directed at the cash register.

The shop should be well lit to attract ch'i into your premises. There should be no dark or gloomy corners where the ch'i can stagnate. Be careful with the glare from afternoon sun. Natural sunlight may seem to be good, but in reality glaring sun brings bad luck and the potential for financial loss. Install anti-glare glass or curtains to counter-act this.

Plants and animals are good for your business, but they need to be looked after. Potted plants or a small aquarium help beneficial ch'i flow throughout your premises. However, if the plants start to droop and the fish begin to die, it is a sign that your business is also dying. Consequently, it is very important to look after them and keep them healthy. Ideally, someone on the staff who likes plants and animals should be given the responsibility of looking after them.

Extreme quiet is just as bad as excessive noise from a feng shui point of view. Play music that is stimulating enough to keep your staff awake and active, but is not too raucous and likely to turn away potential customers.

Your store or office needs to smell fresh at all times. Ensure that there is sufficient ventilation to encourage the ch'i to enter and flow everywhere. Keep your toilets and washrooms out of sight and clean.

The advertising signs for your business also need to fol-low feng shui principles. Naturally, their size should harmo-nize with your premises and not dominate them. The color scheme used should harmonize with your personal element. There are exceptions to this, though. The Chinese fre-quently use red and gold in the color scheme of restaurants. This is because the element of fire is used to cook the food. Red also symbolizes good luck, happiness, and wealth, mak-ing it a good choice for most businesses to use. However, jewelry stores are an example of businesses that should never use red, as fire destroys metal. Instead, jewelry stores are often painted white as this is the color of metal. Times are changing, though, and nowadays it is common to see restaurants and jewelry stores throughout the Orient using a variety of different color schemes.

There is no standard system of colors in feng shui. For instance, some experts say that you should never use black as it represents darkness. However, black also symbolizes water and, as you know, water symbolizes wealth and prosperity.

White is another good example. White is the color of death, but it is also the color of light, and light is good feng shui. White also symbolizes metal, which is gold and silver—wealth and prosperity again.

Red is believed to attract good fortune. Red packets containing money are distributed to employees and children at the time of the Chinese New Year. Chinese brides wear scarlet to attract good luck. Red-painted eggs are distributed to celebrate a baby's first month of life.

Yellow, gold, and green are also considered to be colors that attract good luck. Yellow and gold represent the sun, and green symbolizes spring.

If possible, keep to colors that harmonize with your personal element. These are:

- Fire — red.
- Metal — white.
- Wood — green.
- Earth — yellow.
- Water — black.

You can also choose colors relating to the type of business you are in. For instance, if you are involved in farming or any business that involves wood, green would be a good choice of color to use. Businesses involved with money, such as banks and insurance companies, could use blue or black, as these are the colors of water, which symbolizes money. Realtors could use yellow, as it symbolizes earth.

12

Conclusion

I hope you have enjoyed gaining insight into the fascinating world of feng shui. I found that my whole approach to life altered once I became aware of the importance of living in harmony with the earth. We chose our current home using feng shui and for the first time live in a house that suits every member of the family. We have made changes, both inside and out, to make the home more suitable for our needs, and these were all done using the principles of feng shui.

Feng shui is being utilized more and more around the world and its influence can be seen in unexpected places. Recently, a friend told me that she thought the Sydney Opera House must have been built using feng shui principles. As she looked at the beautiful building situated right on the edge of the harbor, it occurred to her that water is the element of communication and self-expression. The Sydney Opera House is in the perfect position to gain benefit from this element. She also felt that the unusual design and the large amount of glass used enhanced the communication aspects of water. The building exists purely to create beautiful music and could not have been sited in a better location for this purpose.

Experiment with feng shui in every area of your life. Do not expect miracles to happen overnight, but remain quietly confident. Slowly, but steadily, you will notice that your life will improve in many ways, and you will experience much more happiness, abundance, and contentment than ever before. You will discover what an absolute joy life can be when you live in harmony with the earth.

Appendix

Elements and Signs for the Years 1900 to 2000

Element	Sign	Year
Metal	Rat	Jan. 31, 1900 to Feb. 18, 1901
Metal	Ox	Feb. 19, 1901 to Feb. 7, 1902
Water	Tiger	Feb. 8, 1902 to Jan. 28, 1903
Water	Rabbit	Jan. 29, 1903 to Feb. 15, 1904
Wood	Dragon	Feb. 16, 1904 to Feb. 3, 1905
Wood	Snake	Feb. 4, 1905 to Jan. 24, 1906
Fire	Horse	Jan. 15, 1906 to Feb. 12, 1907
Fire	Sheep	Feb. 13, 1907 to Feb. 1, 1908
Earth	Monkey	Feb. 2, 1908 to Jan. 21, 1909
Earth	Rooster	Jan. 22, 1909 to Feb. 9, 1910
Metal	Dog	Feb. 10, 1910 to Jan. 29, 1911
Metal	Boar	Jan. 30, 1911 to Feb. 17, 1912
Water	Rat	Feb. 18, 1912 to Feb. 5, 1913
Water	Ox	Feb. 6, 1913 to Jan. 25, 1914
Wood	Tiger	Jan. 26, 1914 to Feb. 13, 1915

Wood	Rabbit	Feb. 14, 1915 to Feb. 2, 1916
Fire	Dragon	Feb. 3, 1916 to Jan. 22, 1917
Fire	Snake	Jan. 23, 1917 to Feb. 10, 1918
Earth	Horse	Feb. 11, 1918 to Jan. 31, 1919
Earth	Sheep	Feb. 1, 1919 to Feb. 19, 1920
Metal	Monkey	Feb. 20, 1920 to Feb. 7, 1921
Metal	Rooster	Feb. 8, 1921 to Jan. 27, 1922
Water	Dog	Jan. 28, 1922 to Feb. 15, 1923
Water	Boar	Feb. 16, 1923 to Feb. 4, 1924
Wood	Rat	Feb. 5, 1924 to Jan. 24, 1925
Wood	Ox	Jan. 25, 1925 to Feb. 12, 1926
Fire	Tiger	Feb. 13, 1926 to Feb. 1, 1927
Fire	Rabbit	Feb. 2, 1927 to Jan. 22, 1928
Earth	Dragon	Jan. 23, 1928 to Feb. 9, 1929
Earth	Snake	Feb. 10, 1929 to Jan. 29, 1930
Metal	Horse	Jan. 30, 1930 to Feb. 16, 1931
Metal	Sheep	Feb. 17, 1931 to Feb. 5, 1932
Water	Monkey	Feb. 6, 1932 to Jan. 25, 1933
Water	Rooster	Jan. 26, 1933 to Feb. 13, 1934
Wood	Dog	Feb. 14, 1934 to Feb. 3, 1935
Wood	Boar	Feb. 4, 1935 to Jan. 23, 1936
Fire	Rat	Jan. 24, 1936 to Feb. 10, 1937
Fire	Ox	Feb. 11, 1937 to Jan. 30, 1938
Earth	Tiger	Jan. 31, 1938 to Feb. 18, 1939
Earth	Rabbit	Feb. 19, 1939 to Feb. 7, 1940
Metal	Dragon	Feb. 8, 1940 to Jan. 26, 1941
Metal	Snake	Jan. 27, 1941 to Feb. 14, 1942
Water	Horse	Feb. 15, 1942 to Feb. 4, 1943
Water	Sheep	Feb. 5, 1943 to Jan. 24, 1944
Wood	Monkey	Jan. 25, 1944 to Feb. 12, 1945
Wood	Rooster	Feb. 13, 1945 to Feb. 1, 1946
Fire	Dog	Feb. 2, 1946 to Jan. 21, 1947

Fire	Boar	Jan. 22, 1947 to Feb. 9, 1948
Earth	Rat	Feb. 10, 1948 to Jan. 28, 1949
Earth	Ox	Jan. 29, 1949 to Feb. 16, 1950
Metal	Tiger	Feb. 17, 1950 to Feb. 5, 1951
Metal	Rabbit	Feb. 6, 1951 to Jan. 26, 1952
Water	Dragon	Jan. 27, 1952 to Feb. 13, 1953
Water	Snake	Feb. 14, 1953 to Feb. 2, 1954
Wood	Horse	Feb. 3, 1954 to Jan. 23, 1955
Wood	Sheep	Jan. 24, 1955 to Feb. 11, 1956
Fire	Monkey	Feb. 12, 1956 to Jan. 30, 1957
Fire	Rooster	Jan. 31, 1957 to Feb. 17, 1958
Earth	Dog	Feb. 18, 1958 to Feb. 7, 1959
Earth	Boar	Feb. 8, 1959 to Jan. 27, 1960
Metal	Rat	Jan. 28, 1960 to Feb. 14, 1961
Metal	Ox	Feb. 15, 1961 to Feb. 4, 1962
Water	Tiger	Feb. 5, 1962 to Jan. 24, 1963
Water	Rabbit	Jan. 25, 1963 to Feb. 12, 1964
Wood	Dragon	Feb. 13, 1964 to Feb. 1, 1965
Wood	Snake	Feb. 2, 1965 to Jan. 20, 1966
Fire	Horse	Jan. 21, 1966 to Feb. 8, 1967
Fire	Sheep	Feb. 9, 1967 to Jan. 29, 1968
Earth	Monkey	Jan. 30, 1968 to Feb. 16, 1969
Earth	Rooster	Feb. 17, 1969 to Feb. 5, 1970
Metal	Dog	Feb. 6, 1970 to Jan. 26, 1971
Metal	Boar	Jan. 27, 1971 to Jan. 15, 1972
Water	Rat	Jan. 16, 1972 to Feb. 2, 1973
Water	Ox	Feb. 3, 1973 to Jan. 22, 1974
Wood	Tiger	Jan. 23, 1974 to Feb. 10, 1975
Wood	Rabbit	Feb. 11, 1975 to Jan. 30, 1976
Fire	Dragon	Jan. 31, 1976 to Feb. 17, 1977
Fire	Snake	Feb. 18, 1977 to Feb. 6, 1978
Earth	Horse	Feb. 7, 1978 to Jan. 27, 1979

Earth	Sheep	Jan. 28, 1979 to Feb. 15, 1980
Metal	Monkey	Feb. 16, 1980 to Feb. 4, 1981
Metal	Rooster	Feb. 5, 1981 to Jan. 24, 1982
Water	Dog	Jan. 15, 1982 to Feb. 12, 1983
Water	Boar	Feb. 13, 1983 to Feb. 1, 1984
Wood	Rat	Feb. 2, 1984 to Feb. 19, 1985
Wood	Ox	Feb. 20, 1985 to Feb. 8, 1986
Fire	Tiger	Feb. 9, 1986 to Jan. 28, 1987
Fire	Rabbit	Jan. 19, 1987 to Feb. 16, 1988
Earth	Dragon	Feb. 17, 1988 to Feb. 5, 1989
Earth	Snake	Feb. 6, 1989 to Jan. 26, 1990
Metal	Horse	Jan. 27, 1990 to Feb. 14, 1991
Metal	Sheep	Feb. 15, 1991 to Feb. 3, 1992
Water	Monkey	Feb. 4, 1992 to Jan. 22, 1993
Water	Rooster	Jan. 23, 1993 to Feb. 9, 1994
Wood	Dog	Feb. 10, 1994 to Jan. 30, 1995
Wood	Boar	Jan. 31, 1995 to Feb. 18, 1996
Fire	Rat	Feb. 19, 1995 to Feb. 6, 1997
Fire	Ox	Feb. 7, 1997 to Jan. 27, 1998
Earth	Tiger	Jan. 18, 1998 to Feb. 15, 1999
Earth	Rabbit	Feb. 16, 1999 to Feb. 4, 2000
Metal	Dragon	Feb. 5, 2000

Element at Time of Birth

11 P.M.–1 A.M.	Wood	11 A.M.–1 P.M.	Metal
1 A.M.–3 A.M.	Wood	1 P.M.–3 P.M.	Metal
3 A.M.–5 A.M.	Fire	3 P.M.–5 P.M.	Water
5 A.M.–7 A.M.	Fire	5 P.M.–7 P.M.	Water
7 A.M.–9 A.M.	Earth	7 P.M.–9 P.M.	Water
9 A.M.–11 A.M.	Earth	9 P.M.–11 P.M.	Water

Personal Kua for Year of Birth

Chien

Male: 1913, 1922, 1931, 1940, 1949, 1958, 1967, 1976, 1985, 1994
Female: 1919, 1928, 1937, 1946, 1955, 1964, 1973, 1982, 1991

Tui

Male: 1912, 1921, 1930, 1939, 1948, 1957, 1966, 1975, 1984, 1993
Female: 1911, 1920, 1929, 1938, 1947, 1956, 1965, 1974, 1983, 1992

Li

Male: 1910, 1919, 1928, 1937, 1946, 1955, 1964, 1973, 1982, 1991
Female: 1913, 1922, 1931, 1930, 1949, 1958, 1967, 1976, 1985, 1994

Chen

Male: 1916, 1925, 1934, 1943, 1952, 1961, 1970, 1979, 1988, 1997
Female: 1916, 1925, 1934, 1943, 1952, 1961, 1970, 1979, 1988, 1997

Continued on page 166.

Personal Kua for Year of Birth (continued).

Sun

Male: 1915, 1924, 1933, 1942, 1951, 1960, 1969, 1978, 1987, 1996

Female: 1917, 1926, 1935, 1944, 1953, 1962, 1971, 1980, 1989, 1998

K'an

Male: 1918, 1927, 1936, 1945, 1954, 1963, 1972, 1981, 1990, 1999

Female: 1914, 1923, 1932, 1941, 1950, 1959, 1968, 1977, 1986, 1995

Ken

Male: 1911, 1920, 1929, 1938, 1947, 1956, 1965, 1974, 1983, 1992

Female: 1918, 1921, 1927, 1930, 1936, 1939, 1945, 1948, 1954, 1957, 1963, 1966, 1972, 1975, 1981, 1984, 1990, 1993, 1999

K'un

Male: 1914, 1917, 1923, 1926, 1932, 1935, 1941, 1944, 1950, 1953, 1959, 1962, 1968, 1971, 1977, 1980, 1986, 1989

Female: 1915, 1924, 1933, 1942, 1951, 1960, 1969, 1978, 1987, 1996

Central Position Numbers
for the Months of the Year

Approximate dates	Year numbers		
	1, 4, 7	2, 5, 8	3, 6, 9
Dec. 22–Jan. 5	5	2	8
Jan. 6–Feb. 3	4	1	7
Feb. 4–March 5	3	9	6
March 6–April 4	2	8	5
April 5–May 5	1	7	4
May 6–June 5	9	6	3
June 6–July 7	8	5	2
July 8–Aug. 7	7	4	1
Aug. 8–Sept. 7	6	3	9
Sept. 8–Oct. 8	5	2	8
Oct. 9–Nov. 7	4	1	7
Nov. 8–Dec. 7	3	9	6
Dec. 8–Dec. 21	2	8	5

Central Position Numbers for Years 1901 to 2017

9	Fire	1901	1910	1919	1928	1937	1946	1955	1964	1973	1982	1991	2000	2009
8	Earth	1902	1911	1920	1929	1938	1947	1956	1965	1974	1983	1992	2001	2010
7	Metal	1903	1912	1921	1930	1939	1948	1957	1966	1975	1984	1993	2002	2011
6	Metal	1904	1913	1922	1931	1940	1949	1958	1967	1976	1985	1994	2003	2012
5	Earth	1905	1914	1923	1932	1941	1950	1959	1968	1977	1986	1995	2004	2013
4	Wood	1906	1915	1924	1933	1942	1951	1960	1969	1978	1987	1996	2005	2014
3	Wood	1907	1916	1925	1934	1943	1952	1961	1970	1979	1988	1997	2006	2015
2	Earth	1908	1917	1926	1935	1944	1953	1962	1971	1980	1989	1998	2007	2016
1	Water	1909	1918	1927	1936	1945	1954	1963	1972	1981	1990	1999	2008	2017

Notes

Introduction

1. Isabella Bird, *The Yangtze Valley and Beyond* (London: John Murray, 1899; reprint London: Virago Press Limited, 1985), 223.

2. Jan Morris, *Hong Kong* (London: Viking Books, 1988; and New York: Viking Penguin Inc., 1988), 127.

3. Ibid, 127.

4. There is a charming story that explains how Kowloon (Gau lung) got its name. In 1278, the seven-year-old Emperor Di Bing of the Song dynasty was standing on a site across the harbour from the island that was to later become known as Hong Kong. He had fled to this area to escape the Mongols who were invading southern China. Di Bing counted the hills that he could see. There were eight. "Eight dragons," he told the advisor who was with him at the time. The sycophantic advisor shook his head. "There are nine," he said. Ping counted again. "There are eight," he insisted. The advisor

bowed deeply. "Your Imperial Highness is the ninth dragon," he said. Dragons have always been associated with royalty, and the peninsular has been called Kowloon ever since.

5. Kevin Rafferty, *City on the Rocks* (London: Viking Books and New York: Viking Penguin Inc., 1989), 41.

6. Morris, *Hong Kong*, 128.

7. Nina Nelson, *Hong Kong, Macau, and Taiwan* (London: B. T. Batsford Ltd., 1984), 28. Stephen and Stitt guarded the entrance to the old Hongkong and Shanghai Bank building. During the World War II, they were looted by the Japanese during the Occupation and disappeared. They were eventually found in Osaka and returned to their former positions. While they were being reinstated a workman found a bullet hole in one of them, and inside this were some coins. While the new Hongkong and Shanghai Bank building was being constructed the two lions were taken to a secret place that was selected by a feng shui expert.

8. Rafferty, *City on the Rocks*, 41.

9. Lillian Too, *Feng Shui* (Malaysia: Konsep Books, 1993), 110.

10. Rafferty, *City on the Rocks*, 55–56 and 344–345. Feng shui experts still argue about the design of this building, most claiming that it is good feng shui but some insisting that it is bad. The people who claim that it is bad point out the numerous angles that create negative shars for nearby buildings. The people who claim that it is good feng shui point out the excellent location

surrounded by curving roads and flyovers, none of which curve in towards the building. The peaceful Chater Gardens are directly in front of the building, multiplying the availability of ch'i energy.

11. Sally Rodwell, *A Visitor's Guide to Historic Hong Kong* (Hong Kong: The Guidebook Company and the Hong Kong Tourist Association, 1991), 154.

12. *Free China Review* (Vol. 45, No. 4, April 1995), 41.

13. Nancilee Wydra, *Designing Your Happiness* (Torrance, CA: Heian International, Inc.), 15.

14. Frena Bloomfield, *The Book of Chinese Beliefs* (London: Arrow Books Limited, 1983), 21.

15. *A Geography of Hong Kong*, ed. T. N. Chiu and C. L. So (Hong Kong: Oxford University Press, 1983) 59–62. This book contains an article on vegetation by P. Catt.

Chapter 1

1. The story of how Wu of Hsia discovered the tortoise and the different systems of divination that evolved from it is told in Richard Webster's *Talisman Magic* (St. Paul, MN: Llewellyn Publications, 1995).

2. Rodwell, *A Visitor's Guide to Historic Hong Kong*, 17.

3. Evelyn Lip, *Feng Shui: A Layman's Guide to Chinese Geomancy* (originally published as *Chinese Geomancy*, Singapore: Times Editions Private Limited, 1979; American edition Union City, CA: Heian International, Inc, 1987), 3.

4. *The Travels by Marco Polo*, trans. R. Latham (Harmondsworth: Penguin Books Ltd., 1978), 27.

5. Dragons are the first of the four celestial animals in Chinese symbolism. They are also identified with spring, the time of rebirth. Most importantly, from our point of view, dragons are associated with water, one of the most important elements of feng shui. Water, incidentally, is also related to money, and consequently, an ornament of a dragon can constantly motivate its owner to work hard and become wealthy and successful.

6. Edward A. Gargan, "A Symbol of Good Fortune Faces Reshaping," *International Herald Tribune* (Hong Kong edition), June 20, 1995, page 2.

7. A large collection of yin-yang opposites can be found in David Allen Hulse's *The Key of It All, Book One: The Eastern Mysteries* (St. Paul, MN: Llewellyn Publications, 1993), 350–351.

8. Wei Tsuei, *Roots of Chinese Culture and Medicine* (Malaysia: Pelanduk Publications, 1992), 5.

9. Jean-Michel Huon de Kermadec, *The Way to Chinese Astrology*, trans. N. Derek Poulsen (London: Unwin Paperbacks, 1983), 136. The origin of the yin-yang symbol is not known. Some authorities claim it was created by Chou Tun-Yi (1017–1073 C.E.). However, it is likely to be of much older, Taoist origin.

10. Too, *Feng Shui*, 33.

11. Sarah Rossbach, *Feng Shui, the Chinese Art of Placement* (New York: Arkana Books, 1983), 1.

12. As well as a need for burial places for local people, most Chinese want to be buried in their homeland. Consequently, coffins are sent to Hong Kong from around the world. Land is scarce and extremely expensive in Hong Kong. Because of this, most cemeteries lease out their land for seven- or ten-year periods. Once this time is up, the remains are exhumed and cremated. This has deprived the feng shui practitioners of much of their work, and nowadays most of their efforts go into feng shui analysis for the living.

13. Jou, Tsung Hwa, *The Tao of I-Ching.* (Piscataway, NJ: Tai Chi Foundation, 1984), 15. Chin Shih-Huang was the first emperor of the Chin dynasty. He used a variety of measures to unify the country, the most notable being the adoption of a single language. He also attempted to destroy all learning to keep his people ignorant. Consequently, all the scholars of the day were buried alive and all the written works that could be found were destroyed. The I Ching survived this because Chin and his advisors needed its advice for guidance. (Chin Shih-Huang is best remembered for the building of the Great Wall of China, the only man-made structure that can be seen from the moon.)

14. E. A. Crawford and Teresa Kennedy, *Chinese Elemental Astrology* (London: Judy Piatkus [Publishers] Limited, 1992), 46. The productive cycle is very old and is said to have been created by Emperor Huang Ti (c. 2266 B.C.E.), who also invented agriculture, bricks, musical instruments, and much of Chinese philosophy. Huang Ti is considered by the Chinese to be father of the people.

15. Louis Culling, *The Pristine Yi King* (St. Paul, MN: Llewellyn Publications, 1989), 4. King Wen (also frequently known as the Duke of Wen) lived about 1150 B.C.E. and was the first person to give the names of the meanings to the sixty-four hexagrams of the I Ching. He was imprisoned for political reasons and had to be very careful in what he wrote, so as not to further anger his enemies. Consequently, much of his interpretations are deliberately obscure and hard to understand.

16. Information about the elements for hour, day, month, and year of birth can be found in any elementary book on Chinese astrology. I think the best one to start with is *Ming Shu: The Art and Practice of Chinese Astrology* by Derek Walters (New York: Simon and Schuster, Inc., 1987).

Chapter 2

1. Bird, *The Yangtze Valley and Beyond*, 92.

2. J. J. M. de Groot, *The Religious System of China* (Leiden: Brill Verlag, 1897), Volume Three, 951. Feng shui experts today claim that there is always a tiger present near a dragon. However, one hundred years ago it was considered that dragons could exist without a tiger. Dr De Groot wrote: "Dragons and tigers are by no means equally important in the Feng-shui system. Professors are wont to say: 'Any spot is felicitous that has a Dragon and no Tiger; but a spot is not of a certainty unfelicitous if it has only a Tiger and no Dragon.'" Dr de Groot's incredible six-volume work is devoted mainly

to a study of funeral customs. His study of feng shui (Chapter Twelve of Volume Three) has been republished with a commentary in *Chinese Geomancy* by Derek Walters (Dorset: Element Books, 1989).

3. Derham Groves, *Feng Shui and Western Building Ceremonies* (Scotland: Graham Brash [Pte] Ltd., Singapore and Tynron Press, 1991), 13–14. It was not uncommon for artificial hills to be created to act the part of one of the dragon, tiger, tortoise, or phoenix. We have already mentioned the large mound that Marco Polo saw. Coal Hill (Jing-shan) is another man-made mound that was constructed to improve the feng shui of the Forbidden City.

4. Groves, *Feng Shui and Western Building Ceremonies*, 9.

5. Albert Low, *Feng Shui: The Way to Harmony* (Malaysia: Pelanduk Publications, 1993), 18.

6. Richard Webster, *Dowsing for Beginners* (St. Paul, MN: Llewellyn Publications, 1996).

Chapter 3

1. There is some doubt as to the exact dates Wu of Hsia lived. Louis Culling, in his book *The Pristine Yi King* says that the trigrams were doubled up to form the I-Ching hexagrams by 2205 B.C.E. Consequently, the original pa-kua must date from at least 2500 B.C.E.

The Former Heaven arrangement created by Wu is extremely well balanced. Chien (heaven) is in the south position, and K'un (earth) is in the north. This is then followed by Ken (mountain) in the northwest opposite Tui (lake) in the southeast. Chen (thunder) and Sun (wind) come next in the northeast and southwest. The final combination is Li (fire) and K'an (water) in the east and west positions. At first sight they appear to be total opposites. However, according to Wu of Hsia, they keep each other, and consequently the entire arrangement, in balance.

2. Jou, *The Tao of I-Ching*, 27–34.

3. All authorities agree on the importance of the eight locations. They also agree which are the four positive directions and which are negative. However, they disagree on which are the most important. For instance, Mark D. Marfori, in his book *Feng Shui: Discover Money, Health and Love* (California, Dragon Publishing, 1993) considers the prosperity location as being the most positive, followed by health, longevity, and prime. Disaster is listed as being the most important negative location, followed by Six Shar, Five Ghosts, and Death (pages 112–114).

Lillian Too, in her book *Applied Pa-Kua and Lo Shu Feng Shui* (Malaysia: Konsep Books, 1993), says that the Prosperity location is the most favorable, followed by Health, Longevity, and Prime. This agrees with Mr. Marfori, but her negative locations are different. She considers Death to be the worst location, followed by Six Shar, Five Ghosts, and Disaster (pages 67–80).

Chapter 4

1. de Groot, *The Religious System of China* (Brill Verlag, Leiden, 1897), Volume Three, 936.

2. Stephen Skinner, *The Living Earth Manual of Feng-Shui* (London: Routledge and Kegan Paul Limited, 1982. My edition was published in Singapore: Graham Brash [Pte] Ltd., 1983.), 5–6. Chinese geographers have always required that the rivers flow to the east and the highest mountains, where the rivers begin, are sited in the west. Consequently, the warmest, most pleasant place is in the (light-yang) south, and the cold winds originate from the (dark-yin) north. As a result, the pleasant, good south has always been oriented at the top of Chinese maps, with north at the bottom, east at the left and west at the right. Feng shui simply accords with Chinese geography.

   The compass was invented by the Chinese, who used it for many hundreds of years before it became used in the West. The Chinese compass indicated south, rather than north. Up until the seventeenth century, compasses used by surveyors and astronomers in the West also indicated south. Robert K. G. Temple, *China: Land of Discovery and Invention* (Wellingborough: Patrick Stephens, 1986), from the Introduction by Joseph Needham, 7.

3. Joseph Needham, *Science and Civilisation in China* (Cambridge University Press, Cambridge, 1959), Volume Three, 398. At least 2,500 years ago the five main planets had been given descriptive names. Jupiter was

known as "the Year Star," Mars "the Fitful Glitterer," Saturn "the Exorcist," Venus "the Great White One," and Mercury "the Hour Star."

Chapter 5

1. Low, *Feng Shui: The Way to Harmony*, 114.

2. de Groot, *The Religious System of China*, 968–969. Often the twenty-four seasons have their own special circle on the luo-pan. The different divisions are named in typically Chinese lyrical terms. First we have spring, divided into: Beginning of Spring, Rain Water, Resurrection of Hibernating Insects, Vernal Equinox, Pure Brightness, and Rains Over the Grain. Then comes summer: Beginning of Summer, Grain Filling a Little, Grain in Ear, Summer Solstice, Slight Heat, and Great Heat. This is followed by autumn: Beginning of Autumn, Limit of Heat, White Dew, Autumnal Equinox, Cold Dew, and Descent of Hoar Frost. Finally we have winter: Beginning of Winter, Little Snow, Heavy Snow, Winter Solstice, Little Cold, and Severe Cold.

3. English language luo-pans are available from the American Feng Shui Institute, 108 North Ynez Avenue, Suite 202, Monterey Park, CA 91754.

Chapter 6

1. Albert Low, *Practical Feng Shui for the Home* (Malaysia: Pelanduk Publications, 1995), 436.

2. In the days of the Mandarins, people had to pass the "Official" examinations to gain promotion in the bureaucracy. The term is still used in Chinese astrology as one of the five forces of Fate, Seal, Wealth, Opportunity, and Official, and is related to success in examinations and public life.

3. Low, *Feng Shui: The Way to Harmony*, 105–106.

4. Lillian Too, *Practical Applications of Feng Shui* (Malaysia, Konsep Books, 1993), 145. It is believed to be bad feng shui to install an indoor pool in your home on the right-hand side of the front door when you are looking out. This is believed to give the husband a "roving eye" and to encourage infidelity. Consequently, install any indoor pool on the left-hand side. This is also a good side from a wealth and prosperity point of view.

Chapter 7

1. Groves, *Feng-shui and Western Building Ceremonies*, 24.

2. Too, *Applied Pa-Kua and Lo Shu Feng Shui*, 117–123.

Chapter 10

1. Philippa Waring, *The Way of Feng-Shui* (Souvenir Press Limited, London, 1993), 100.

2. Reverend M. Yates, a missionary, recorded in *The Chinese Recorder and Missionary Journal* of 1868 that pagodas were erected to improve feng shui. "My interpreter explained that it (the pagoda) had been erected by the

local villagers in the hope of improving their Fung Shui. If their crops were good in successive years, if no pestilence descended upon them, and if, above all, their people should live in harmony and prosperity, then the experiment in Fung Shui would be declared a success." A year earlier, Mr Yates related an interesting story to the Missionary Quarterly Meeting in Shanghai. "During the time the rebels occupied the city of Shanghai, the Yamen (official residence) of the district magistrate was destroyed. A short time previous to this a magistrate had died, and his death was attributed by the Fung-shui professor to my church tower, which was due North of the Yamen. It must be borne in mind that the influence of Fung-shui, when undisturbed, proceeds in a line due North and South. When the rebels left the city, and the local authorities were about to resume their old positions, they sent to me a deputation to consult in regard to pulling down my church tower, stating as a reason that it had been the cause of one magistrate's death, and consequently no one was willing to serve while this exposed." This was a major problem that was only resolved when a feng shui expert came up with the simple solution of rebuilding the Yamen at an angle to its original position. "Thus, as the murderous spirit proceeds due South, when it passes the corner of the wall, its course will diverge from the end wall and no evil influence can possible follow." The Yamen was rebuilt and no magistrate had died there since. (Recorded in de Groot, *The Religious System of China*, Volume Three, 1042–1043.)

Glossary

Chen — Chen is one of the eight trigrams that make up the sixty-four hexagrams of the I Ching, and is represented by two broken yin lines above a straight yang line. It symbolizes decision-making. It also governs health and family matters.

Ch'i — Ch'i is pure energy, the universal life force that exists in every living thing. In feng shui, it is regarded as being the dragon's breath. Ch'i energy is gathered and cultivated to bring good fortune and happiness to the people fortunate enough to live in its presence. Ch'i must have freedom to move, otherwise it becomes stagnant and any good fortune dissipates. In windy areas, ch'i is quickly scattered and lost, making these places unfavorable in feng shui terms.

Chien — Chien is one of the eight trigrams, and is represented by three straight yang lines. It symbolizes activity, energy, and perseverance. It governs mentors and other useful people.

Compass School — There are two main schools of feng shui, the Form School and the Compass School. The Compass School uses the pa-kua, the eight trigrams of the I Ching, and Chinese astrology to assist in making calculations. It uses a more technical approach than that adopted by the Form School. In practice today, most feng shui practitioners use a combination of both schools in making their assessments.

Cycle of Birth — The five elements of Chinese astrology create three different cycles. The Cycle of Birth is a positive, productive one where each of the elements assists in supporting and creating the element that follows it in the cycle. The cycle is: fire, earth, metal, water, wood. It then starts again with fire. Fire produces earth. Earth produces metal. Metal liquifies, symbolizing water. Water nourishes wood. Finally, wood burns to create fire.

Cycle of Destruction — The five elements of Chinese astrology can be arranged to create a destructive cycle with each element overpowering and dominating the element that follows it in the cycle. In this arrangement, fire is able to melt metal. Metal can destroy wood. Wood draws its strength from the earth. Earth is able to dam and block water. Water is able to put out fire.

Cycle of Reduction — The five elements of Chinese astrology can be arranged in a cycle to remedy the unfortunate results of the Cycle of Destruction. In the Cycle of Reduction, fire burns wood. Wood absorbs water. Water corrodes metal. Metal comes out of the earth. Finally, earth is able to to put out fire. In practice, the Cycle of Reduction is used to reduce the strength of different elements. If someone has too much fire, for example, the addition of earth reduces the effects of this potentially negative element.

Dragon — The dragon is the most revered mythological animal in China. The dragon's influence in feng shui is immeasurable, and dragons are featured in all of the earliest books on the subject. Master Yang Yun Sang wrote a trilogy of books in the ninth century C.E. that explained in great detail how to locate and make good use of the dragon. Favorable and unfavorable sites in feng shui are determined by dragon symbolism. According to the teachings of the Form School, wherever a dragon is found, there will also be a tiger. Dragons are found in hills and mountains, and are discovered by analyzing the land formations, the quality of the vegetation and the sweetness of the air. Dragons are not found on flat land or steep hills.

East Four Houses — The East Four Houses are derived from the eight directions indicated by the eight-sided pakua. There are four east houses and also four west houses. The east ones are Li, K'an, Chen, and Sun. If your house has a back door that faces south, you are living in a Li house, which has an element of fire. The four east houses are summarized this way:

House	Back door faces	Element
Li	South	Fire
K'an	North	Water
Chen	East	Wood
Sun	Southeast	Wood

Feng Shui — Feng shui literally means "wind and water." It is the art and practice of living in harmony with the earth. In feng shui it is believed that if you choose the right place to live and work, your life will be filled with joy and abundance. If we live in harmony with the winds and the waters of the earth we can create happy, positive lives for ourselves.

Feng shui has a history going back many thousands of years. For most of its history it was practiced solely in the East and was regarded as a superstitious practice in the West. In the twentieth century it expanded around the globe and is more popular today than at any other time in its history.

Five Elements — In feng shui, we use the five elements of Chinese astrology—fire, earth, metal, water, and wood. Each element has its own distinct energy and the different combinations of elements play an important part in feng shui. The different elements can either harmonize (as in the Cycle of Birth) or oppose (as in the Cycle of Destruction) other elements.

Flying Star — The Flying Star system of feng shui studies the auspicious and inauspicious times of a building for any given period. Consequently, it is possible to determine the trends ahead of time and take appropriate action.

Form School — In feng shui there are two major schools: the Compass School and the Form School. As the name indicates, the Form School looks at different sites and evaluates them for the quality and quantity of ch'i energy. A good site would contain both the green dragon and the white tiger. Consequently, in the Form School, the most emphasis is placed on the shapes and orientations of hills, mountains, streams, and rivers.

Geomancer's Compass — The geomancer's compass (generally known as the luo-pan) is the compass used for determining directions in the Compass School of feng shui. The luo-pan consists of a compass surrounded by a number of circles containing information that is used in feng shui. Usually, everything is contained in a square base plate. The edge of the plate is aligned with a wall of the building enabling accurate directions to be taken from the compass.

I Ching — The I Ching or "Book of Changes" is China's oldest book and was originally devised by Wu of Hsia in 3322 B.C.E. The I Ching has had a profound effect on Chinese culture and civilization. Throughout its history scholars, emperors, and generals have consulted it before making important decisions. Its importance was such that when Chin Shih-Huang ordered the destruction of all the books in China in 215 B.C.E. he excepted just one book, the I Ching. This was because he and his advisers could not rule the country without its guidance.

The I Ching is an oracle containing sixty-four different symbols known as hexagrams. Each hexagram consists of six lines, which are either straight or broken. Consequently, there are sixty-four possible combinations. The hexagrams are made up of two trigrams, one on top of the other. The hexagrams can be used for both divination and meditation.

K'an — K'an is one of the eight trigrams and is represented by a straight yang line between two broken yin
lines. It symbolizes secrets and craftiness. It governs
career and opportunities.

Ken — Ken is one of the eight trigrams and is represented
by a straight yang line above two broken yin lines. It rules
the study or learning area of the home.

K'un — K'un is one of the eight trigrams and is represented by three broken yin lines. It symbolizes receptive-
ness and devotion. It governs marriage.

Lao Tzu — Lao Tzu lived about 600 B.C.E. and was the
founder of Taoism. The name Lao Tzu means "old boy."
This name was given to him as it is believed that he was
born with white hair. His main philosophy was to let
things take their natural course because matters would
always work out without effort.

Li — Li is one of the eight trigrams and is represented by a
broken yin line between two straight yang lines. It symbolizes beauty, light, and fire. It governs fame and reputation.

Lo Shu — *See* magic square.

Luo-Pan — *See* geomancer's compass.

Magic Square — A magic square consists of a series of
numbers arranged inside a grid where all the horizontal,
vertical, and diagonal rows add up to the same number.
Magic squares have been popular in China since Wu of
Hsia found one in the markings of a tortoise shell. His discovery formed the basis of the I Ching, Chinese astrology,

the Ki, Kigaku, Chinese numerology, and feng shui. The pa-kua of feng shui utilizes the same magic square that Wu discovered thousands of years ago to determine the positions of the eight trigrams.

Pa-Kua — The pa-kua is an extremely powerful symbol of Chinese culture and is frequently found hanging over doors of Chinese households as a symbol of protection. It is eight-sided in shape and usually has either a mirror or the yin-yang symbol in the center. Around this center are arranged the eight trigrams of the I Ching.

The pa-kua indicates the eight compass directions and the trigrams also relate to the five elements. By using the pa-kua we can determine a person's most auspicious and inauspicious directions and locations.

Remedies — Remedies are any method used to modify or eliminate harmful effects caused by shars or imbalances in the five elements. For instance, a fence could act as a remedy if it blocked a poison arrow.

Shars — Shars, often known as "poison arrows," are negative energies that carry bad luck and misfortune. They travel in straight lines and can be created in many ways. A straight road heading towards a house facing a T-junction would be considered a shar. An angle created by two walls of a neighbouring house pointing in your direction would also be considered a shar.

Sun — Sun is one of the eight trigrams and is represented by two straight yang lines above a broken yin line. It symbolizes strength of character. It governs wealth and prosperity.

Tui — Tui is one of the eight trigrams and is represented by a broken yin line above two straight yang lines. It symbolizes spiritual matters. It governs children.

Tortoise — Tortoises have always been considered a symbol of longevity and happiness. The ancient Chinese believed that gods lived in the shells of turtles and tortoises, so the appearance of the giant tortoise crawling out of the Yellow River when Wu of Hsia was working on improving the irrigation was a remarkably good omen. It was only later that Wu discovered the three-by-three magic square in the shell's markings, and this ultimately led to the art and science of feng shui.

Trigrams — The eight trigrams comprise every possible combination of straight and broken lines that can be constructed into three lines. The straight lines are called yang lines and represent male energy. The broken lines are known as yin lines and represent female energy. The hexagrams in the I Ching consist of two trigrams, one on top of the other. The trigrams date from the time of Wu of Hsia and are believed to contain all the wisdom of the universe. The national flag of South Korea contains all eight trigrams, showing that they are still considered to be just as important today as they were in the time of Wu.

West Four Houses — The West Four Houses are derived from the eight directions indicated by the eight-sided pa-kua. There are four east houses as well as four west houses. The west houses are: Chien, K'un, Ken, and Tui. If the back door of your house faces west, you are

living in a Tui house, which has an element of metal.
The four west houses are summarized this way:

House	Back door faces	Element
Chien	Northwest	Metal
K'un	Southwest	Earth
Ken	Northeast	Earth
Tui	West	Metal

Wu of Hsia — Emperor Wu of Hsia (sometimes referred
to as Fu Hsi) was the first ruler of China and is believed to
have lived some 4,800 years ago. He was the first of the
five legendary emperors of that period. No one knows if
he actually existed, but he has been credited with many
discoveries, including the tortoise that contained the
magic square on its back. Consequently, he is regarded as
being the father of feng shui, the I Ching, Chinese astrology, and numerology, and the other systems that have
derived from these.

Yin and Yang — Yin and yang represent opposites in the
Taoist philosophy. For instance, black is yin and white is
yang. North is yin, south is yang. Night is yin, day is yang.
In this system everything can be considered as being
either male or female. Yin is female, yang is male. The
concept originally came from two sides of a mountain.
The yin side was the shady, northern side, and yang was
the sunny, southern side. This dualistic view of the universe plays an important role in feng shui.

Suggested Reading

Carus, Paul. *Chinese Astrology*. La Salle, IL: Open Court, 1974.

Crawford, E. A. and Teresa Kennedy. *Chinese Elemental Astrology*. London: Judy Piatkus (Publishers) Ltd., 1992.

Culling, Louis T. *The Pristine Yi King*. St. Paul, MN: Llewellyn Publications, 1989.

Eitel, Ernest J. *Feng-Shui*. Singapore: Graham Brash (Pte) Ltd., 1985.

Groves, Derham. *Feng-Shui and Western Building Ceremonies*. Singapore: Graham Brash (Pte) Ltd. and Scotland: Tynron Press, 1991.

Hean-Tatt, Ong. *The Chinese Pakua*. Malaysia: Pelanduk Publications, 1991.

Kushi, Michio (with Edward Esko). *Nine Star Ki*. Becket, MA: One Peaceful World Press, 1991.

Lip, Evelyn. *Feng Shui: A Layman's Guide to Chinese Geomancy*. Union City, CA: Heian International, Inc., 1987.

Lo, Raymond. *Feng-shui and Destiny*. Lutterworth, UK: Tynron Press, 1992.

Low, Albert. *Feng Shui: The Way to Harmony*. Malaysia: Pelanduk Publications, 1993.

Marfori, Mark D. *Feng Shui: Discover Money, Health and Love*. Santa Monica, CA: Dragon Publishing, 1993.

Needham, Joseph. *Science and Civilisation in China* (Volume Two and Volume Four). Cambridge: Cambridge University Press, 1959.

Rossbach, Sarah. *Feng Shui, The Chinese Art of Placement*. New York: E. P. Dutton, 1983.

—————. *Interior Design with Feng Shui*. New York: E. P. Dutton, 1987.

Skinner, Stephen. *The Living Earth Manual of Feng-Shui*. London: Routledge and Kegan Paul Ltd., 1982.

Temple, Robert. *China: Land of Discovery and Invention*. Wellingborough: Patrick Stephens Limited, 1986. (Published in the U.S.A. as *The Genius of China*, New York: Simon and Schuster, 1986.)

Too, Lillian. *Feng Shui*. Malaysia: Konsep Books, 1993.

Index

For Readers of
Feng Shui for Beginners

Free
Feng Shui Mapping Guide!

Thank you for purchasing *Feng Shui for Beginners*. After reading this book, you will want to immediately apply the techniques of this time-honored tradition for improving your home and work environment. You will be amazed at the profound effects that the simple art of placement will bring into your life. Llewellyn is offering readers of *Feng Shui for Beginners* a free Feng Shui Mapping Guide–a transparent pa-kua to lay over any floor plan so you can determine the most favorable areas of health, prosperity, and happiness. Fill out this order form and send it in today. Hurry, quantities are limited.

No photocopies accepted. Please use this form only.
Please Print

Full Name_____

Mailing Address_____

City, State, Zip_____

Complete and mail this form, plus $1.50 for shipping, to:

Llewellyn Publications,
Feng Shui Mapping Guide Offer
P. O. Box 64383, Dept. K803-6
St. Paul, MN 55164-0383

Allow 4-6 weeks for delivery

Llewellyn publishes hundreds of books
on your favorite subjects.

LOOK FOR THE CRESCENT MOON
to find the one you've been searching for!

To find the book you've been searching for, just call or write for a FREE copy of our full-color catalog, *New Worlds of Mind & Spirit*. *New Worlds* is brimming with books and other resources to help you develop your magical and spiritual potential to the fullest! Explore over 80 exciting pages that include:

- **Exclusive interviews, articles and "how-tos" by Llewellyn's expert authors**

- **Features on classic Llewellyn books**

- **Tasty previews of Llewellyn's latest books on astrology, Tarot, Wicca, shamanism, magick, the paranormal, spirituality, mythology, alternative health and healing, and more**

- **Monthly horoscopes by Gloria Star**

- **Plus special offers available only to *New Worlds* readers**

To get your free *New Worlds* catalog, call
1-800-THE MOON

or send your name and address to

Llewellyn
P.O. Box 64383,
St. Paul, MN 55164–0383

Many bookstores carry
New Worlds—ask for it! Visit our
web site at www.llewellyn.com.

LLEWELLYN
New Worlds of Mind and Spirit